LAW ENFORCEMENT
MEMORABILIA

Price And Identification Guide

Monty McCord

Published by

krause publications

700 E. State Street • Iola, WI 54990-0001

Please call or write for our free catalog. Our toll-free number to place an order or obtain a free catalog is 800-258-0929 or please use our regular business telephone 715-445-2214 for editorial comment and further information.

Library of Congress Catalog Number: 98-87373
ISBN: 0-87341-697-X
Printed in the United States of America

Photos by author unless otherwise noted.

DEDICATION

Dedicated to the thousands of American law enforcement officers who have died in the line of duty wearing their "silver stars and gold shields."

"Greater love hath no man than this, That a Man lay down his Life for His Friends"
...JOHN 15:13

Officer Joel R. Conklin, Badge #17,
Killed in the line of duty,
October 9, 1993

ACKNOWLEDGMENTS

A book of this type would not be possible without the assistance of outside sources. I would like to thank the Nebraska State Patrol Academy and Lt. Darrell Fischer for allowing me to photograph the collection housed there. I am very grateful to Mr. Steve Knight, M.A., Los Angeles County Marshal's Department-Retired, for allowing me to include his comprehensive badge hallmark list. My appreciation also goes to the National Association of Chiefs of Police for allowing me to reproduce one of their magazine covers. Others who furnished photos and information; Don Vessey, James Post, Clarence Gibson, Greg Reynolds, Terry Jessee, Texas D.P.S. Texas Rangers, U.S. Marshals Service, Lincoln, NE Police Dept., Indiana State Police, V.H. Blackinton & Co. Inc., Revell-Monogram Inc., AMT-ERTL Co., Lindberg Models, Jo-Han Models, Yodel, Matchbox, Liberty Classics Inc., to whom I'm truly thankful.

Thanks to Les Bugai, Jr. for allowing me to photograph some of his restraints, and to Les Bugai, Jr. and Daniel Geary for letting me photograph their John Behan sheriff badge and for supplying such helpful and necessary information.

And last but not least, Debra and Tracy Conklin, who allowed me to photograph Joel's badge, so he could be part of the dedication of this book, thank you....

CONTENTS

INTRODUCTION

I have enjoyed the hobby of collecting police memorabilia for more than twenty years. In that time, I've established many friendships worldwide. For me, these contacts have been as rewarding as finding the badges for my collection. The collecting of law badges dates back to the early twentieth century, when officers themselves kept the badges they used throughout their careers. These treasures were usually handed down through the family. Generally speaking, those not in police work, didn't have access to badges. A Los Angeles County Deputy Sheriff, Vincent J. Monteleone, is known as one of the first official badge collectors. He started his collection in 1919 while serving as a Deputy U.S. Marshal and died with a collection of around 750 badges.

Across the country, law enforcement agencies grew and likewise more and more badges were produced. Badges started showing up on estate sales, flea markets and with antique dealers. Over the last 30 years civilians were able to formally start collecting. I have located badges for my collection in various places, from gun shows, relatives, military collectors, non-collector friends, and coin dealers to name a few.

The purpose for a book of this type is multifold. It will formally introduce the hobby of collecting police memorabilia and illustrate most of the primary areas being collected today. By no means does it cover every collectible law enforcement item that exists.

This book will provide reference material to gun, antique, military and other dealers/collectors who don't normally deal in police items. It will give value ranges of various collectibles in order for them to price them accurately. Many times prices are guesstimates at best, and in many cases it's unknown for sure whether a given item is authentic or a reproduction—especially with badges. Many aren't aware that law enforcement memorabilia collecting has been an organized hobby since the early 1970s with the establishment of the first collector's association. The hobby received the first comprehensive monthly publication in 1982 when *Police Collector's News* (PCNEWS) was first published.

Many times collectors are the victims of unscrupulous people who sell them "Grandpa Leroy's police badge that he wore in the 1890s." The high quality of reproduction badges today makes unethical dealing possible, on both sides. On one occasion, while looking through the tables at a gun show, I noticed what appeared

to be an old shield with cut out star badge that read, "U.S. Marshal." I recognized it from a catalog of high quality reproduction badges. Since I'm interested in U.S. Marshal badges real or reproduction, I inquired about the price.

The gun dealer stated, "$150, it's the real thing." I knew that this badge sold for about $50 in the catalog. I asked if he had any documentation on it, and he told me that he bought it with the old revolver and holster that the badge was pinned onto. He must have felt that this qualified as documentation.

In reality, if this badge was genuine, (and documented), it would have been worth between $350-$450. Also, if it actually had some connection with the gun and holster, it would have been very foolish to break up the set, which would have been worth much more together. Once I realized that he was firm on the story of the badge being genuine, I thanked him for his time and moved on.

This book will allow both expert and novice collectors to gain insight into the types of badges available, guidelines for valuations, what badges are rare and tips on establishing the authenticity of badges. This will help collectors avoid those who offer badges or other items at inflated prices.

A word to the wise—acquire badge catalogs, photocopied lists of other collectors and especially catalogs of reproduction badges so one can become familiar with what's available.

The hobby offers a fascinating glimpse into police history, whether you collect only one area, or all types of law enforcement items. Interestingly, a recent non-official poll indicated what the top three most popular police collectibles were. It wasn't surprising that badges were first and patches second, but third place went to miniature police vehicles! The growth of this area has been nothing short of phenomenal, with die-cast companies producing wide varieties of vehicles in scales from 1/64 to 1/18. Some of these die-casts are coin banks and some are limited editions. The plastic model kit manufacturers currently offer an unsurpassed selection of police kits.

Never before in history, have there been more plastic model police car kits than now. A cottage industry of after-market items has been born which offers a multitude of decals and equipment which enables modelers to build many variations of police vehicles using these existing kits.

CHAPTER I

BRIEF HISTORY OF BADGES & COLLECTING

The origin of the police badge can be traced to the heraldic designs from the Middle Ages. However, for the purpose of this work, we will start with the period most familiar to us, the time when use of the badge started becoming a visible identifier for the man enforcing the law. This period of our history is the mid-19th century. Even though most of us consider this era when the badge first became common, it was fairly rare for the frontier peace officer to have one. More often than not, if the frontier town marshal wanted a badge, he strolled over to the refuse pile, picked out a tin can or drinking cup, and crudely fashioned himself a star to wear. This is where the term, "tin star" originated.

On occasion, the local blacksmith or silversmith would fashion a badge for use. Later, as the western frontier became more populated, badge and jewelry manufacturers sent "drummers" or traveling salesmen to sell their wares. They would carry stock badges with them that carried basic titles such as, "Marshal", "Deputy", or "Sheriff."

An example of a shield with pierced 5-point star. Kearney, NE, police. **Value: $40-$60**

They also carried badge blanks and were equipped with the tools to hand stamp the lettering the customer desired. Mail order catalogs from companies in San Francisco, Los Angeles, Denver, Kansas City and St. Louis were also a source for the lawman's badge. The 1886 Peck & Snyder "Sporting Goods" catalog offered a variety of circle 5-point stars, shields with cut-out stars, plain shields and suspension badges, all in the $.50 to $2.00 range!

During the late 1880s, badges that were a little fancier, such as those surmounted with an eagle, appeared. The plain styles were the most commonly used through the Old West period on up into the 1930s. It should be noted, that these same "plain" styles are currently available from some manufacturers.

They have had to move over for the newer styles of shields such as the eagle top heart-shape and the oval, as well as the fancier and heavier stars. These new styles come adorned with a variety of options such as a choice of finishes, full-color state center seals and hard enamel or reverse enamel lettering on the panels for example.

Ordering a badge today could compare to ordering a new car, because there are so many options available. Of course, as with cars, options add to the badge's original cost. Collectors of modern badges watch for these options which add value to the badge. Badges that are semi-custom or full custom die (not available in catalog) are usually much more impressive than catalog badges and command a higher price.

Other items a collector may look for that would add to the value of a badge would be a hallmark, or maker's identification stamp located on the back of the badge. Hallmarks sometimes help to authenticate and identify the age of a badge. Inscriptions on the backs of badges may also assist in identifying who used it and when.

As I mentioned in the introduction, the organized hobby has been around for many years. Regional police collector meets are held around the country and abroad. These meets are just like gun or antique shows, except the tables are covered with just about every piece of law enforcement memorabilia you could imagine! It's also a great place to meet new friends who are interested in the same hobby that you are. The meets are held all over the country, and are hosted by collectors who live in that area. If you're only able to attend one meet a year, it should be the national. Nowhere on earth will you see as many collectors, badges, patches, photos, uniforms, headgear, reading material, miniature and full-size police cars and related items than at the national meet.

The first national meet was held in Los Angeles, CA in 1985. Since then, they have been in: Piscataway, NJ-1986; Chicago, IL-1987; Denver, CO-1988; Washington, D.C.1989; Louisville, KY-1990; Kansas City, MO-1991; Reno, NV-1992; Lancaster, PA-1993; Reno, NV-1994; Marlborough, MA-1995; Arlington, TX-1996; St. Louis, MO-1997; and Denver, CO-1998. The variety of locales gives just about every collector a chance to attend a national meet at least once or twice. The national meet is the place to encounter many foreign collectors who fly in to attend.

Because of the huge number of law enforcement agencies, it is common for a collector to choose a topic or area to collect. For example,

one may seek only badges from his/her home state, or a particular agency. I've known collectors that specialized only in police, sheriff, state patrol, federal or railroad police badges. The choices are almost limitless.

A word to the wise here, when I started collecting in 1974, I collected everything, which included all types of law badges. This led to some degree of frustration as it seemed like I had no direction in my collecting. Unable to narrow my interest down to only one area, I at least chose a few more manageable ones.

This isn't to say that I will pass up a badge if it does not fall into one of my interest areas—because a collector always needs trading stock. Anyone has the freedom to collect whatever they want. The bottom line is to enjoy doing it!

Nowadays law badge collectors are not only law enforcement personnel, but civilians as well. It should be mentioned here, that there is a growing concern for the illegal use of police badges. It's not uncommon anymore to see an article in the newspaper where someone used a badge in a crime. Legitimate collectors are not usually those responsible for those crimes—but we take the heat for them. Because of those who falsely represent themselves as police officers, in order to carry out a crime, the hobby suffers from new laws being passed. Collector's sources are also drying up because of real or imagined liabilities.

Collectors and dealers should deal with those they know to be legitimate collectors. A worst case scenario would be to trade or sell a badge to someone you don't know, and have that person use the badge to enable him to harm an innocent person. Antique, gun, and other dealers are in a position where it would be common not to know every customer they sell to. Civilians should know that a real officer should display not only his badge, but a photo identification card as well.

A person giving a quick 'flip' of a wallet, allowing only a glimpse of the badge, should be asked to see the badge and ID close up. A variety of high-quality, generic "security officer" badges are readily available, which, at a glance look like the real thing. It is important to note here that laws are in effect in certain states that limit or prohibit the possession of law enforcement insignia. Be sure to check your state laws so you

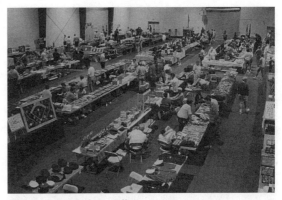

The national police collector conventions established in 1985, and continue to grow each year. This photo shows a portion of the huge 1991 Kansas City National convention.

This U.S. Marshal shield with pierced star is a very nice reproduction, but not worth the $150 asking price of a gun dealer.   **Value: $10-$40**

This plain 6-point star, known as a "stock" badge, is a good example of the badges traveling drummers had to offer local towns.   **Value: $75-$150**

By the 1880s, shields topped with the American eagle came into use. This style commanded a hefty $2 in 1886.   **Value: $45-$60**

A variety of stock titles were available from traveling salesmen. This example is a "City Marshall"
Value: $80-$175

A plain 6-point star with balled tips features the title and county name.   **Value: $75-$100**

Circle 5-point stars were very popular during the Old West, and still are to some extent. This example is handmade and hand lettered. This Arapahoe appears to have hand-engraved lettering.
Value: $185-$250

A handsome 6-point star which is adorned with extra stamped designs as well as an engraved border. This fine example was used by a patrolman in Hannibal, Missouri from 1892 to 1901.
Value: $200-$275

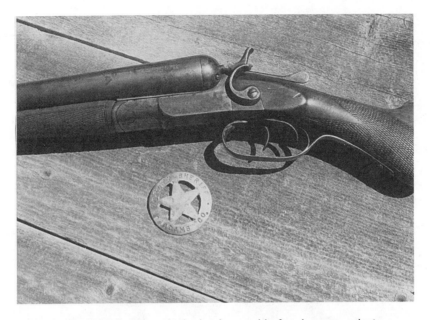

If the frontier lawman wanted a badge, he would often have to make it himself out of whatever was available, like tin cans. They were fittingly termed "tin stars." **Value: $500+**

The conventions feature many collectors who display their fine collections. They usually have trade/sale items which are used to acquire new additions to their collection.

This collector appears to specialize in major city and state patrol badges.

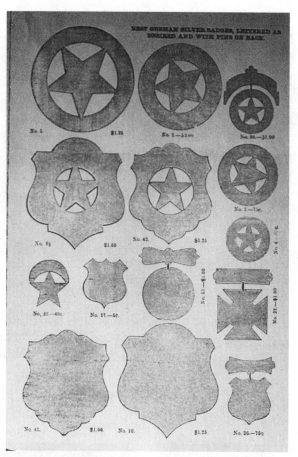

A sample page from the 1886 Peck & Snyder *Sporting Goods* catalog shows a variety of popular styles. The large circle star sold for $1.25.

This impressive collection centers on cap badges, helmets, helmet plates (badges) and rank epaulets from England.

Specialized collections are those that are collected from a certain department, county, state, time period, etc. The collection above are antique badges from the Kansas City, Mo. police department.

Badges are often displayed with shoulder patches from the same agencies.

This photo, taken about the turn-of-the-century, shows a style of uniform known affectionately as the "Keystone Cop" uniform.

Many collectors specialize in certain areas, such as this fine set of Kansas City, Mo. patrolman badges used through the years.

Various badges from the Kansas City, KS Police Dept.

Generic security guard badges are easy to obtain. They look very official if flashed quickly in one's face.
Value: $10-$15

An ornate 5-point star, lettered simply, "Deputy Sheriff." **Value: $45-$65**

A unique plain shield with embossed edges and ornate designs. **Value: $45-$65**

A nice example of an 1880s-1890s shield with pierced star, this one used by the Lincoln, Nebraska police. **Value: $150-$225**

Shield with pierced star lettered simply, "Special Police." **Value: $35-$45**

Harold Welding, Sheriff of Cuming County, Ne., from 1959 to 1989, used this circle 5-point star.
Value: $55-$70

This old shield shows areas where the nickel plating is worn off. Good sign of actual use.
Value: $35-$50

Two examples of hat badges that are a little more valuable because acency names appear as well as their age. The Sergeant badge has a miniature Salt Lake City Police badge for a center seal. The San Antonio Police was used in the early 1900s.
Value: $15-$18 $55-$65
(left)   (right)

The first badge I acquired for my collection in 1974; I thought the $3 asking price was a little high!
Value: $75-$85

This circle 5-point star features a fine engraved design on the star. Note the unusual spelling of "Marshal" with two "L"s. The badge was used in the 1920s.
Value: $150-$200

Exceptional and unusual lettering style was used
on this plain 6-point balled-tip star.

Value: $30-$35

1940s-1950s vintage, plain shield from
Grant County Nebraska. **Value: $55-$75**

Plain 6-point balled-tip star with simple
"Special Officer" designation. **Value: $25-$30**

Another example of a stock badge shield with
pierced star reads simply, "Deputy Sheriff."
This style originally sold for $1.50.

Value: $75-$90

The "wreath" style badge was popular with
police from the late nineteenth and early twentieth
centuries. Usually a hat badge, it appeared on many
of the "keystone cop" style helmets. It featured
applied letters and numbers which denoted rank,
badge number or simply the term "police.

Value: $50-$75

CHAPTER 2

BASIC BADGE TYPES
AND STYLES

If a collector or dealer wants to have some basic knowledge about law badges, they should be familiar with the types and styles that have been and are currently available. Manufacturing processes are different which make some badges heavy and some lightweight. Naturally a badge's weight is affected by the material it is made from—such as solid gold! The attachments on the back of badges called "jewelers findings" will tell where the badge was meant to be worn. For example, a badge with a screw or post is normally used on a hat. The familiar pin-type is for use on shirts or coats and can be mounted on leather holders that snap onto the belt. The wallet clip looks much like a money clip except it is not as wide. Clip back badges are used in a wallet or badge/ID case. Some badges, utilized to hold paper currency, have the wider money clip on back.

Clutch-back fasteners that are usually seen on nameplates, and rank and collar insignias are sometimes used on badges. They can be attached

This eagle-top shield has a "Police" marked center seal instead of the usual state seal. **Value: $25-$35**

to a shirt or cap. These back attachments tell what type of badge you have: pin back—breast badge; post back—hat badge; clip back—wallet badge; clutch-back—breast or hat badge. Other parts, or options on a badge are:

Finishes:

Nickel plating: surface of raw material (usually brass) of badge is plated with nickel .

Rhodium: Platinum-based silver metal plated over nickel base.

Rho-Glo: (by V.H. Blackinton) is a solid silver metal which requires no plating.

Gold plate: Depending on the manufacturer, a 14-22k gold plate applied to badge.

Hi-Glo: (By V.H. Blackinton) A solid gold-colored metal which requires no plating.

Two-tone: Badge that has both silver and gold, for example gold panels and silver back, or vice-versa.

Gold-filled: Most companies offer gold-filled badges. These contain varying amounts of actual gold content.

Sterling Silver: A silver alloy that is usually about 92% genuine silver.

Note: There exist many more finishes offered by companies which are variations of the above listed finishes, but often using a specially registered brand name for them. Special order badges can be made of solid gold, or silver.

New finishes offered by V.H. Blackinton & Co. are: "Rose Gold"—a look of old gold; "Black"—an all black badge for SWAT type use and "Bronze"—which gives an antique bronze look.

Center Seals:

A wide variety of types and sizes exist, the most common being state seals. Seals are available plain with no lettered rim, plain with lettered rim, plain with enamel lettered rim, full color enamel with no lettered rim or full-color enamel with lettered rim. State seals with lettered rim will read either, "State of," or, "Great Seal of the State of." Other seals include plain stars, stock designs, military seals and duty specialties to name a few. Custom-designed center seals have become very popular. Usually these are the official seals of the city or county, but sometimes they depict an historic object, i.e. building.

Panels:

Panels are the surfaces either applied to the badge or are a part of the badge that contain the lettering. Panels can be plain metal like the badge where the lettering is stamped in and then painted (soft enamel), or the lettering can be stamped in and filled to the letter's surface with enamel and then baked (hard fired enamel). Another type is the reverse enamel panel where the lettering is raised, enamelling is filled to the level of the letters, and hard fired. The basic variety of enamel colors are; red, white, blue, black, green, yellow, and brown.

Letter Style:

Lettering styles vary among manufacturers, but they all are variations of two major styles,

Block or Roman. Block is a plain style, with Roman being a fancier style of lettering. Many antique badges were hand-engraved, which sometimes resulted in beautiful, unique lettering. The number of different badge styles available today is staggering. Large and small companies offer catalogs with hundreds of styles. Some of these companies have been around since the nineteenth century and still offer the old plain styles.

At the turn-of-the-century, many more styles were added which have become the mainstay catalog badges of today. Many of these styles are offered by a handful of companies, some with only minor differences. These badges can simply be picked out of the catalog and ordered with the desired lettering, center seals and back attachments. The catalog badge (the badge most commonly encountered) is considered lower in value than a semi-custom or total custom die badge. Many things determine the value of a badge, however, which we'll be discussing later on.

A small number of badge manufacturers offer styles different than regular catalog types. These would be of greater interest to most collectors.

Most badge manufacturers offer semi to total custom die badges, designed either by the customer or the company. Handmade badges are very valuable because of the craftmanship as well as the material used. Some handmade badges are crafted from coins or the backs of pocket watches and sometimes have precious stones mounted on them. Oftentimes, special presentation badges of yesteryear were handmade. These generally command very high prices depending on the material (gold, sterling silver etc.) and type of gems used. As explained in Chapter One, frontier lawmen did sometimes make their own badges or had the local blacksmith or silversmith make one. These would be extremely valuable today.

A Deputy Sheriff shield from Denver, Colorado, which features a money clip attachment on the back. The deputy's name, "Geo. Brewton," is on the top pane.

A "wire pin" shown on the back of this shield.

This pre-1940 shield features a variation of the "Fielding" type catch.

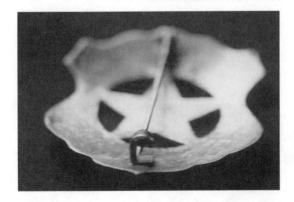

An example of the "tongue" catch, first used around the turn-of-the-century.

An example of the "Burgess Safety Catch," first patented in 1909 and is the most popular catch used today.

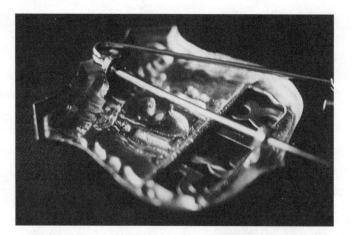

"Bar Post Mounts" are used primarily on the backs of eastern police shields. This NYPD shield shows how the large safety pin passes through the two bar posts, and then the pin can be fastened.

A variation of a tube-type catch, which covers the end of the pin.

Unlike the Burgess catch that has a rotating ring inside the hook, the outside of this catch rotates.

A medium-sized 5-point star with a wallet clipback for
use in a badge/ID case or regular wallet.

Not commonly found on badge backs, are the clutch-
back fasteners which are commonly used on nameplates, collar insignia, etc. This example is a U.S. Navy
Master-At-Arms badge.

The screw or "post" back is mainly used on hat
badges. The post back was first used in the 1880s
on army hat badges.

The pin was removed from this 6-point star and a metal strip
soldered onto the back to allow the badge to be worn on the belt.

Massachusetts-style, sometimes called an "arm & hammer" shield, features an enamel rim state seal and soft-enamel block letters. **Value: $30-$35**

Sunburst style with full-color enamel custom city seal and soft-enamel block letters.
Value: $35-$45

Eagle-top sunburst with enamel rim, state seal, and soft-enamel block letters. **Value: $30-$35**

A 7-point star with State of Colorado seal.
Value: $70-$80

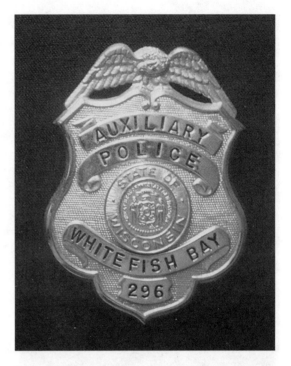

Example of an "auxiliary" marked eagle-top shield, with plain Wisconsin state seal.   **Value: $20-$25**

Wreath-sided round shield with full-color state seal and soft block letters.   **Value: $25-$30**

This Mobile, Alabama shield has a custom city seal that was made by a reverse stamp process. Note the badge's back and how the city seal was stamped from behind, raising the design and lettering on the front.   **Value: $75-$90**

6-point balled-tip star with color state seal and soft-enamel block lettering.   **Value: $25-$35**

This pre-1940 Omaha Police badge is a total custom die done in the reverse stamp process.
Value: $150-$175

7-point star with color state seal and soft-enamel block lettering.   **Value: $25-$35**

5-point balled-tip star with full-color enamel state seal, and soft-enamel block letters.
Value: $35-$45

8-point star (1880s-1890s) with applied copper numbers and soft-enamel letters.
Value: $200-$250

Eagle-top shield with applied copper numbers and soft-enamel block letters. **Value: $85-$100**

Plain crescent 5-point star with soft-enamel lettering. **Value: $30-$45**

Total custom die oval shield with color enamel city seal and hard enamel block letters.
Value: $150-$175

Another unusual badge is this New York City "Special Patrolman" which is a round custom die badge with cut-out numbers. **Value: $35-$40**

Eagle-top teardrop shield with full-color Great Seal of New Mexico and hard-enamel roman lettering. Bottom panel features a design stamp.
Value: $85-$100

Eagle-top shield from Missouri features a plain state seal. This "Deputy Marshal" shield was used in the 1950s. **Value: $45-$65**

An unusual custom die shield, this civilian Pittsburg PD shield is a circular belt and buckle shape. Regular officer's badges feature applied copper numbers to the center. **Value: $60-$70**

CHAPTER 3

HALLMARKS

Webster's New World Dictionary defines "hallmark" as "an official mark stamped on British gold and silver articles originating at Goldsmith's Hall in London, as a guarantee of genuineness; any mark or symbol of genuineness or high quality." Badge makers began stamping the name of their business, or "hallmark" on the backs of badges sometime around the 1850s. If you have a badge with a hallmark, it is an added bonus because it can be used to help date the badge.

This chapter includes photo examples of what some hallmarks look like as well as an invaluable list of hallmarks dating back to the mid 19th century. It should assist in identifying approximately when and where a badge was made.

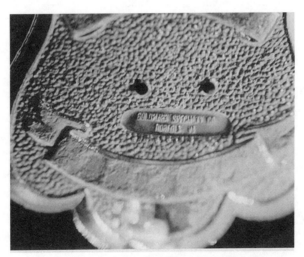

"Goldmark Specialty Co. Norfolk, VA."

The following exhaustive hallmark list was researched and written by retired Los Angeles County Marshal, Steven Wayne Knight. It took Mr. Knight several years to develop this list which was done by searching old manufacturer's lists at libraries and interviewing many current badge makers. He searched badge books for hallmarks which included old badge company histories. He inspected badges at many national and state collectors shows and collected papers and old books that mentioned badges. The list represents more than 500 hours of Mr. Knight's diligent and painstaking work. I am indebted to him for his permission to use his list in my book.

Hallmark Listing

Maker's Mark (as appears on badge)	Location	Year(s)	Additional	City/State
A. A. UNLITE	——	Old unknown	City HM	Philadelphia, PA
A. A. WHITE	157 Westminister St.	Unknown	——	Providence, RI
ABBOTT CO.	76 Spring St.	1949	——	New York, NY
A. B. C. TRAFFIC SIGNAL	——	1937-39	HM, Listed Co.	Scranton, PA
A. B. C. TRAFFIC SIGNAL	——	1949	Move listed	Dunmore, PA
A. BERBERIAN	174 Chestnut	Unkn-1944	——	Providence, RI
A. C. GIBSON CO.	74 Oak St.	1937-39	——	Buffalo, NY
A. C. GIBSON CO.	Oak-Eagle Bldg.	1949-69	——	Buffalo, NY
ACME CO.	1020 Broadway	1935	——	Oakland, CA
ACORN BADGE CO.	35 S. Dearborn	1949	——	Chicago 3, IL
ACROMARK CO.	7-15 Morell St.	1949	——	Elizabeth, NJ
ADAMS CO., S.G.	411 N. 6th	1937	——	St. Louis, MO
ADAMS CO., S.G.	960 Olive St.	1949	——	St. Louis, MO
ADCRAFT CO.	233 Broadway	1930	——	NY, NY
ADCRAFT MFG. CO.	2448 W. Cermak	1937-39	——	Chicago, IL
ADCRAFT MFG. CO.	3324 W. Cermak	1949	——	Chicago, IL
A.F.B. CO.	——	1855-1870	1st LA Sheriff Mfg.	L. A., CA
A.J. DENNISON & CO.	——	1937-49	Listed Co.	Riverside, RI
ALBERT SAMUELS CO.	——	1920-40	Jewelry HM	San Francisco, CA
ALL CITIES UNIFORM	994 Madison Ave.	1992-Present	——	Paterson, NJ
ALLEN	——	Unkn.	Hallmark	New York
ALLEN BROS.	55 Cornhill	1880s	——	Boston, MA
ALLEN DOANE & CO.	29 & 31 Cornhill	1900s	——	Boston, MA
ALLEN DOANE & CO.	15 Wharf	1949	——	Boston, MA
ALLEN JAMES & CO.	——	1937	Listed Co.	Charleston, SC
RITTER CO.	2922 S. Main	1939	——	L. A., CA
ALLEN STAMP & SEAL CO.	——	Unkn-1939	City HM	Kansas City, MO
ALLEN STAMP & SEAL CO.	——	1880-1937	City HM	Kansas City, MO
ALLEN STAMP & SEAL CO.	——	1937-Present	Still there	Kansas City, MO
AMCO (in diamond)	Unknown	1940s	Badges	——
AMERICAN BADGE CO.	LaSalle & Hubbard	1899-1950s		Chicago, IL
AMERICAN BADGE CO.	Chicago 10, IL.	1949	Listed Co.	
AMERICAN BADGE CO.	——	1965-Present	Plastic badges	Yoncalla, OR
AMERICAN BADGE CO.	149 23rd N.	1909-11	——	Portland, OR
AMERICAN BADGE CO.	495 Washington	1911-1913	Out of Bus.	——
AMERICAN EMBLEM CO.	——	1937-39	Listed Co.	Utica, NY
AMERICAN EMBLEM CO.	Earle St.	1949	——	Utica, NY
AMERICAN EMBLEM CO.	——	1928-50s	See Above	Utica, NY
AMERICAN FLAG & BAN	125 N. Dearborn	1949		Chicago, IL
AMERICAN LAFRANCE	Unknown	Unknown	Hallmark	
AMERICAN METAL CRAFTS CO.	——	1937-39	——	Attleboro, MA
AMERICAN PACIFIC STAMP CO.	——	1930-64	Out of Bus.	L.A., CA
AMERICAN PACIFIC	——	1930-64	Badges	L. A., CA
AMERICAN RAILWAY SUPL	——	Unkn.	City HM	New York, NY
AMERICAN SEAL & STAMP	32 S. Clark	1939-49	——	Chicago, IL
AMERICAN SPECIALTIES	5112 4th Ave.	1944	——	Brooklyn, NY
AMERICAN STAMP WKS.	——	1940s	Badges	Dayton, OH
AMERICAN SUPPLY CO.	——	Unknown	City HM	New York, NY
AMES JEWELRY CO.	——	1937 & 39	Badges	Ames, IA
AMES PLATING CORP.	——	1937 & 39	Badges	Chicopee, MA
ANGELL MFG CO INC.	1250 E. Monument	1937-49	Badges	
APRIL MFG. CO.	——	1987-Present	Badges	Industry, CA
ARCUS TICKET CO.	348 1N. Ashland	1949	——	Chicago, IL
ARMSTRONG & VERNIER	——	1897-1898	Old Company	Toledo, OH

Hallmark Listing

Maker's Mark (as appears on badge)	Location	Year(s)	Additional	City/State
ART BURNSIDE	——	1940-70	City HM	Spokane, WA
ARTHUR LIMERICK CO.	202 W. Chase	1939	——	Baltimore, MD
ARTHUR STAFFORD CO.	——	Unkn.	See N. STAFFORD	New York, NY
ARTUNIAN JLRS.	——	Unkn.	City HM	L. A., CA
ATC UNIFORMS	43-58 11th St.	1992-Present	——	Long Island, NY
AUGUST C. FRANK	732 Shannon	1939	——	Philadelphia, PA
AULD CO., D.L.	6th & 5th St.	1939-49	——	Columbus, OH
A.W. MITCHELL & CO.	——	Unkn.	Hallmark	Boston, MA
BAINBRIDGE, C.J.	——	1949	Badges	Syracuse, NY
BAIRD CO.	——	1980s	by IRVINE JACHENS	Chino, CA
BAKER & RICARD	——	1896-1897	Old Company	Toledo, OH
BANNERMAN	——	Unkn	Hallmark	New York
BANNING STAMP & STEN	——	1944 & 49	Badges	Syracuse, NY
BASCH & CO. , L.	——	1907-11	Badges	Toledo, OH
BASTIAN BROS. CO.	1941 Bastian	1949	——	Rochester, NY
BASTIAN BROS. CO.	——	1895-Present	Badges	Rochester, NY
BASTAIN BROS. CO.	223 Broadway	1937 & 39	——	New York, NY
BASTIAN	——	1950-Present	City/State HM	Geneva, NY
BATES	225 N Broad St.	1939	——	Elizabeth, NJ
B.C. STAMP WORKS	——	Unkn.	City HM	Vancouver, B. C.
BEDISHIMER & CO., I.	12 & Sansom	1937 & 39	——	Philadelphia, PA
BEDISHIMER & CO., I.	1210 W. Sansom	1949	——	Philadelphia, PA
BENJ. HARRIS CO. INC.	229 Bowery	1939	——	New York, NY
BENNENT PTG, & STAMP	Bennent Bldg.	1949	——	Atlanta, GA
BERBERIAN CO., A.	174 Chestnut	1944	——	Providence, RI
BERKS JEWELRY CO.	——	1937	Listed Co.	Reading, PA
BERNARD & CO., F.A.	175 5th Ave.	1937 & 39	——	New York, NY
BEST STAMP CO.	——	1880-1928	Hand Engraved Bdges	New York, NY
BEST STAMP CO.	——	Unkn.	City/State HM	Kansas City, MO
BEST STAMP Co.	——	1920-1940	City/State HM	Kansas City, MO
BEST STAMP & MFG. CO.	812 Delaware	1937-1938	——	Kansas City, MO
BEST STAMP & MFG. CO.	900 Main	1939-49	——	Kansas City, MO
BLACKINTON	——	1865-Present	1860s 1st badges	Attleboro, Ma.
BNB PHOENIX, AZ.	Noted Hallmark	1980-Present	See next below	See next below
BNB BADGES	——	1980-Present	By V.&V. Mfg.	Industry, Ca.
BOARDMAN RUBBER STAMP CO. OH.		1884-1896	Founding name	
BOARDMAN STAMP CO.,	——	1896-1968	See SUPERIOR	Toledo, OH
BOARDMAN'S SUPERIOR STAMP CO.,OH		1917-1919	Name HM	
BOARDMAN STAMP CO.	——	1937 & 49	Listed Co.	Toledo, OH
BOSTON BADGE CO.	294 Wash'n St.	Unkn.	——	Boston, MA
BOSTON REGALIA CO.	76 Summer	1937 & 39	——	Boston, MA
BOSTON REGALIA CO.	600 Washington	1949	——	Boston, MA
BOSTON STENCIL & STAMP	7 Broad St.	1937 & 39	——	Boston, MA
BRADSHAW	93 Lafayette	1937 & 39	——	Newark, NJ
BRAKMEIER BROS.	121 S. 4th Ave.	1929-1950s	——	Louisville, KY
BRAXMAR, C.G.	47 Cortland, NY	1879-1890	Address HM	
BRAXMAR CO.	——	1937 & 49	NY Hallmark	New York, NY
BRAXMAR, NY	36 Cortland	1879-1890	Address HM	——
BRAXMAR, NY	47 Cortland	1890-1900	Address HM	——
BRAXMAR, NY	10 Maiden Lane	1900-1910	Address HM	——
BRAXMAR, NY	10-12 Maiden	1910-1926	Address HM	——
BRAXMAR, NY	242 W.55th St.	1926-1948	Address HM	——
BRAXMAR CO., C.G.	242 W.55th St.	1939	Address HM	——
BRAXMAR, NY	216 E. 45th St.	1948-Present	Address HM	——

Hallmark Listing

Maker's Mark (as appears on badge)	Location	Year(s)	Additional	City/State
BUCHLEIN & SCHNEIDER	Newark, NJ	Unkn.	See L. SCHNEIDER	——
BUCHLEIN & SCHNEIDER	252 Market St.	1937 & 39	——	Newark, NJ
BUCHLEIN DIV.ENGRAV	1010 Broad St.	1992-Present	——	Newark, NJ
BUNTING STAMP C	310 Blvd. of Allies	1869-1939	——	Pittsburgh, PA
BUNTING STAMP C	312 Blvd. of Allies	1939-1955	——	Pittsburgh, PA
C. ENTENMANN	——	1928	See ENTENMANN	Los Angeles, CA
CADILLAC STAMP CO.	2138 Riopelle	1937	——	Detroit, MI
CADILLAC STAMP CO.	Riopelle & Neville	1939	——	Detroit, MI
CADILLAC STAMP CO.	2140 Riopelle	1949	——	Detroit, MI
CAIRNS & BROS.	——	1840-1870	City/State HM	New York, NY
CAIRNS & BRO.	Grand St.	1870-1890	Street HM	New York, NY
CAIRNS & BRO.	——	1890-1920	City/State HM	New York, NY
CAIRNS & BROS.	444 Lafayette	1937-39	——	New York, NY
CAIRNS & BROS.	——	1949-Present	No longer mfg.	Clifton, NJ
C.A. KLINKER & CO.	——	1889-1893	Badges until death	San Franscisco, CA
CALDWELL STAMP MNF., CO.	——	1920-21	Badges	Toledo, OH
CALIFORNIA NOVELTY CO.	921 Broadway	1902-04	——	Oakland, CA
CALTROCO	——	1950-79	CAL TROPHY CO	San Franscisco, CA
CAL STAMP	——	1890-1934	Out of bus	San Diego, CA
CAL TROPHY	——	Unkn.	City(abbr.)HM	San Francisco, CA
CAL TROPHY	——	Unkn.	City HM	San Francisco, CA
CANNEFF, J.J.	——	1864-1886	Badges	Toledo, OH
CAR ENTENMANN JLY	1018 Venice LA	1919-1968	Jewelry Co. add.	
CARL ENTENMANN & S	——	1930-1939	1888 mfg. jewelry	L. A., CA
CARLTONE	——	1939-Present	See ENTENMANN	L. A., CA
CARNARVON	Unkn.	1910s	MT & TX badges	——
CARNES STAMP CO.	——	Unkn.	See Gus Messing	St. Paul, MN
CARNES STAMP CO.	315 Jackson	1949		St. Paul, MN
CARRAGAN & TILSON	——	1860-1883	Everson-Ross bought	New York, NY
CARROLL CO., J.B.	Albany & Carroll	1902-1950	——	Chicago, IL
CATHEDRAL ART METAL CO.	15 Gordon	1939	——	Providence, RI
C.D. REESE	22 Nassau St.	Old unkn.	On POLICE badge	New York, NY
C.D. REESE	57 Warren, NY	1930-1939	See S.H. REESE	New York, NY
C.D. REESE	67 Warren, NY	Unkn.	Variation	New York, NY
CELLOMET PRODUCTS	——	1939	Badges	New York, NY
CENTRAL MONOGRAM WKS.	7 W. Madison	1939	——	Chicago, IL
CENTRE FIREARMS	——	Old unkn.	Both states HM	NY- NJ
CENTURY RUBBER STAMP WKS	553 Pearl	1937 & 39	——	New York, NY
C.G. BRAXMAR	47 Cortland	1879-1890	Address HM	New York, NY
C.G. BRAXMAR	242 W. 55th St.	1939	——	New York, NY
CHANDLER & FISHER CO	——	1939	Listed Co.	Cleveland, OH
CHAS. DYER BROS & CO	234 Mass Ave.	1939	——	Indianapolis, IN
CHAS. D. REESE	57 Warren	1939	——	New York, NY
CHASE, ARTHUR	——	1917-1931	Badges	Toledo, OH
CHAS. GREENBLATT	——	Old unkn.	City (abbr.)HM	N. Y. C., NY
CHAS. SCHWEIZER CO	223-229 Russell	1939		St. Louis, MO
CHATTANOOGA BUTTON & BADGE	109 E 7th St.	1937 & 49	——	Tenn.
C.H. DAWSON	Ohio	Unkn.	Hallmark	
CHICAGO RUBBER STAMP	865 Broadway	1908-1910		Oakland, CA HM
CHICAGO RUBBER STAMP	721-930 Broadway	1912-1915		Oakland, CA HM
CHICAGO RUBBER STAMP	1752 Broadway	1915-1924		Oakland, CA HM
CHICAGO RUBBER STAMP	1020 Broadway	1924		Oakland, CA HM
CHICAGO UNIFORM & CAP	208 W. Moore	1937 & 39	——	Chicago, IL

Hallmark Listing

Maker's Mark (as appears on badge)	Location	Year(s)	Additional	City/State
CHIGACO UNIFORM CAP	162 N Franklin	1949	——	Chicago, IL
C.H. HANSON	——	1866-1987	Bought by Blackinton	
C.H. HANSON CO.	303 W. Erie	1937 & 49	——	Chicago, IL
CHILDS & CO, S. D.	17 No. Loomis	1937 & 49	——	Chicago, IL
CHIPRON RUBBER STAMP	126 S. Spring	1892-1910	Founded see NOBLE	——
CHIPRON RUBBER STAMP	224 W. First	1910-1942	Address HM	——
CHIPRON STAMP CO.	224 W. First	1949	Bought by LAS&SCO	——
CHIPRON STAMP & STAT	1620 S. Hill	1952-68	LAS&SCO named it	——
C.H. KOSTER CO.	79 Mercer	1937	——	New York, NY
C.H. MORSE & SON	21 N. Water St.	1939	——	Rochester, NY
CINCINNATI REGALIA CO.	14 W. 4th	1937 & 39	——	Cincinnati, OH
C. J. BAINBRIDGE	——	1949	Badges	Syracuse, NY
CLEVELAND METAL STP	——	Old unkn.	No longer mfg.	Cleveland, OH
CLOVER CO., F.G.	139 Charles St.	1879-1950s	NY 14, NY	——
CLOVER CO., G.	——	1940s	City HM	New York, NY
COLORADO BADGE & NOV.	1523 Tremont	1937	——	Denver, CO
COLORADO BADGE & NOV.	1435 Welton	1939	——	Denver, CO
COLORADO BADGE & NOV.	2051 Champs	1949	——	Denver, CO
COLUMBIA STAMP WKS	418 S. Dearborn	1937 & 39	——	Chicago, IL
COLUMBIA STAMP & ST	431 S. Dearborn	1949	——	Chicago, IL
COLUMBUS STAMP WKS.	——	1937 & 49	Badges	Columbus, OH
CONSOLIDATED STAMP MFG	15 Dey	1949	——	New York, NY
CONSOLIDATED STAMP MFG	56 Church	1992-Present	——	Spring Valley, NY
COOK CO., H.T.	——	1852-1887	Died & Co. sold	Toledo, OH
CRAFTERS INC.	14 S. Jefferson	1949	——	Chicago, IL
CRUVER MFG. CO.	2470 W. Jackson	1937 & 39	——	Chicago, IL
CUNNINGHAM CO., M.E.	100 E Carson	1937 & 39	——	Pittsburgh, PA
CURRY, SAMUEL F.	44 N. 4th St.	1937 & 39	——	Philadelphia, PA
CURRY INC, SAMUEL F	231 Chestnut	1949	——	Philadelphia, PA
CUSTOM INSIGNIA	by: V & V MFG.	1980s	See "BNB"	——
C.W. NIELSEN	——	1971-Present	City/State HM	Chehalis, WA
DARLEY & CO, W.S.	2812 W. Wash.	1949	——	Chicago, IL
DARLING CO., J.C.	——	1937	Listed Co.	Topeka, KS
DAUGHTERY STAMP CO	217 W First	1906-10	Merged CHIPRON	——
DAVIDSONS SONS, JOS.	210 S. 13th	1937 & 49	——	Philadelphia, PA
DAWSON, C.H.	——	Unkn.	Hallmark	Ohio
DAWSON CO. MFG.	——	Unkn.	City/State HM	Cleveland, OH
DAWSON CO. MFRS.	3620 Superior	Unkn.-Present	——	Cleveland, OH
DAYTON STENCIL WKS.	113 E. 2nd St.	1937 &49	——	Dayton, OH
DAYTON STENCIL WKS.	——	1919-1963	Badges	Dayton, OH
DAYTON STENCIL WKS, THE	——	1895-Present	1963, NLM Badges	Dayton, OH
DEANE & ADAMS CO.	——	Unkn.	Old Brass Co.	London, England
DECORATIVE POSTER CO.	2126 Bennett	1939	——	Cincinnati, OH
D. E. JOHNSON CO.	164 W. 22nd St.	1937 & 39	——	New York, NY
DEMOULIN BROS. & CO.	1018 S. 4th St.	1937 & 49	——	Greenville, IL
DENNISON & CO., A.J.	——	1937 & 49	Listed Co.	Riverside, RI
DENVER NOVELTY WKS.	——	1890-1893	HM, See KAUFMAN	Denver, CO
DESIGNS BY CHAMBERLAIN	3105 S. 122nd	1978-Present	ST, Omaha, NE	Omaha, NE
DES MOINES RUBBER STAMP	——	Unkn.	See PIONEER CO.	Iowa
DETECTIVE PUBL CO.	1029 S. Wabash	1937 & 39	——	Chicago, IL
DETECTIVE PUBL CO.	845 S. Wabash	1949	——	Chicago, IL
DETROIT RUBBER STAMP CO.	Michigan	1890-Unkn	——	Detroit, MI
DETROIT STAMP & STEN	523 Shelby	1949	——	Detroit, MI
DICKEY-GRABLER C	10208 Madison Ave.	1937 & 49	——	Cleveland, OH

Hallmark Listing

Maker's Mark (as appears on badge)	Location	Year(s)	Additional	City/State
DIEGES & CLUST INC.	15 John St.	1937	——	New York, NY
DIEGES & CLUST INC.	17 John St.	1939 & 49	——	New York, NY
DIEGES & CLUST MKRS, N.Y., NY		1915-1950s	Badges	New York, NY
DIXIE SEAL & STAMP	——	1937 & 39	Badges	Atlanta, GA
DIXIE SEAL & STAMP	Dixie Bldg.	1949	——	Atlanta, GA
D. L. AULD CO.	6th & 5th Streets	1939-1949	——	Columbus, OH
DODGE INC.	706 N. Hudson	1949	——	Chicago, IL
DONALD LAVIGNE INC.	——	Unkn.	City/State HM	Miami, FL
DORMEY & CO. P.	528 Walnut	1937 & 39	——	Cincinnati, OH
DORST-CINNI	Cincinnati, OH	1900-Present	——	Cincinnati, OH
DUCKGEISHEL	——	Unkn.	Name HM	Chicago, IL
DURY & FINNEY	——	1900-1915	Name HM	Nashville, TN
DYER CO., CHAS.	234 Mass. Ave.	1937 & 49	——	Indianapolis, IN
EAGLE REGALIA CORP.	298 Broadway	1912-1950s	NY 7, NY	New York, NY
E. & H. SIMON INC.	381 4th Ave.	1949	——	New York, NY
E.A.G. ROULSTON	——	1853-Unkn	6pt star for PD	Boston, MA
ECONOMY NOV. & PTG.	227 W 39th St.	1944-1949	——	New York, NY
E.C. SHAW CO.	312 Main St.	1937 & 49	——	Cincinnati, OH
EDELMAN'S	——	Unkn.	Name HM	Farmingdale, NY
ED JONES	——	1897-1906	Part-time maker	Oakland, CA
ED JONES	——	1906-1970	Left IRVINE-JACHE	Oakland, CA
ED JONES	41st St.	1900-1910	Address HM	——
ED JONES	906 Broadway	1910-1915	Address HM	——
ED JONES	1901 Broadway	1915-1923	Address HM	——
ED JONES & CO. MAKERS	20 Broadway	1923-1940	Variation HM	——
ED JONES & CO.	——	1923-1970	Many Variations	Oakland, CA
ED JONES CO., THE	537 16th St.	1970-Present	——	Oakland, CA
ED SMITH STENCIL WKS	Natchez Alley	1867-1927	——	New Orleans, LA
ED SMITH STENCIL WKS	416 Camp St.	1927-1960	Moved	——
ED SMITH STENCIL WKS	326 Camp St.	1960-Present	See NOPD & ESSW	——
EDWARD R. ROEHM	15 E. Grand River	1939	——	Detroit, MI
EDW. H. SCHLECHTER	——	1939	Listed Co.	Allentown, PA
EDW. K. TYRON CO.	——	1920s	City HM	Philadelphia, PA
E.G. STAATS & CO.	——	1937 & 49	Badges	——
E.J. LEIFF MFG. CO.	——	Unkn.	Badges	Salt Lake, UT
E.J. TOWLE	——	1932-1981	City HM See W.E.	Seattle, WA
E.J. TOWLE CO.	——	1932-1981	City HM See W.E.	Seattle, WA
ELECTRIC SVS. SUPLS	2901 N 17th St.	1937 & 49	——	Philadelphia, PA
EMBLEM & BADGE CO.	220 Eddy	1944	——	Providence, RI
EMECO	Unkn.	1880-1920	U.S. Marshals HM	——
ENGLES	Unkn.	Unkn.	Name HM	——
ENTENMANN (1st form)	1018 Venice	1928	Half Circle HM	——
ENTENMANN L. A.	——	1940-1968	See C. ENTENMANN	L. A., CA
ENTENMANN L. A.	L. A. 15, CA	1943-1962	Before zip codes	——
ENTENMANN & SONS	——	1940-1968	ROVIN '68 partner	L. A., CA
ENTENMANN ROVIN CO.	4747 Citrus	1968-Present	——	Pico Rivera, CA
ES (current NYPD off-duty shield)	——	1990-Present	See SHERRY & "NY"	——
ESSW	New Orleans, LA	1867-1970s	See ED SMITH STEN	——
ETCHED PRODUCTS CORP	3901 Queens	1949	——	Long Island, NY
EVANS & CONVERY	24 N. 6th St.	1937	——	Philadelphia, PA
EVANS & CONVERY	6th & Sedley	1939	——	Philadelphia, PA
EVANS & CONVERY	20 N. 6th St.	1949	——	Philadelphia, PA
EVERARD & CO.	——	1910s	Name HM, a jobber	Pasadena, CA
EVERSON-ROSS NY,NY MEYER & WENTHE		1883-1973	Bought it in '73	——

Hallmark Listing

Maker's Mark (as appears on badge)	Location	Year(s)	Additional	City/State
EVERSON-ROSS CO.	88 Chambers St.	1905-1950s	——	New York, NY
EVERSON-ROSS CO.	44 Warren St.	1950-1967	——	NY, NY -Moved
EVERSON-ROSS CO.	15 West St.	1967-1987	——	Spring Valley, NY
EVERSON-ROSS CO.	56 Church St.	1987-Present	——	Spring Valley, NY
E. ROSS GOLD BEAM	Only HM	Unkn.-Present	EVERSON-ROSS HM	——
E. ROSS SIL BEAM	Only HM	Unkn.-Present	EVERSON-ROSS HM	——
EXCELSIOR	——	1895-1965	City/State HM	——
EXCELSIOR STAMP	W. 15 Euclid Arcade	1949	——	Cleveland, OH
EXCELSIOR	——	1965-Present	Original HM used	Stow, OH
F.A. BERNARD & C.	175 5th Ave.	1939	——	New York, NY
FEDERAL I. D.	——	1949	Listed Co.	OK City, OK
FEELEY INC., W.J.	181 Eddy St.	1937	——	Providence, RI
FEELEY & CO., JAS. R.	53 Clifford	1944-1949	——	Providence, RI
F.G. CLOVER CO.	139 Charles St.	1930-1940s	——	New York, NY
F.H. NOBEL & CO.	555 W. 59th St.	1939	——	Chicago, IL
FIFTH AVE UNIFORM CO	19 S. Wells	1940-Unkn	——	Chicago, IL
FISCH & CO.	2816 S. San Pedro	1937	——	L. A., CA
F. JOS MULHAUPT & SONS	Lafayette	1939	Listed in IN.	——
F.J. MANLEY	370 E. 149th St.	1920s	——	NY City, NY HM
F.J. MULHAUPT	——	1910	City/State HM	Lafayette, IN
FLAGER	——	1939	Badges	Atlanta, GA
FLOODING CO.	——	1939	Badges	Atlanta, GA
F.N. WILCOX	——	1920s	City/State HM	Oak Park, IL
FOLGER STEPHEN, LANE	180 Broadway	1937 & 49	——	New York, NY
FORCE CO, WM. A.	222 Nichols Ave.	1949	——	Brooklyn, NY
FOX CO.	3400 Beekman	1937 & 49	——	Cincinnati, OH
FOX STAMP CO.	——	1900-1950	GUSTAVE FOX,NLM	——
FRANK, AUGUST C.	732 Shannon	1937 & 39	——	Philadelphia, PA
FRATERNITY JWLY MFG	Cedar Rapids	Unkn.	Iowa, HM	——
FRED C. KAUTZ & CO.	2634 W. Lake	1937 & 39	——	Chicago, IL
FREEMAN, JACOB	——	1877-1932	Toledo badges	Toledo, OH
FREEMAN	——	1877-1886	Name HM	Toledo, OH
FREEMAN, J.J.	——	1886-1895	Name HM	Toledo, OH
FREEMAN & CO, J.J.	——	1895-1908	Name HM	Toledo, OH
FREEMAN INC., J.J.	——	1908-1930	Name HM	Toledo, OH
FRESNO RUBBER STAMP CO	1039 "J" St.	1892-1893	——	Fresno, CA
FRESNO RUBBER STAMP	1923 Fresno St.	1913-1919	Listed Co.	——
FULLER REGALIA & COSTUME CO.		1937 & 39	——	Worcester, MA
G. CLOVER CO.	——	1940s	City HM	New York, NY
G.J. MAYER CO.	——	Unkn.	City(abbr.)HM	Indianapolis, IN
GARD CO.	——	Unkn.	Name HM	Worcester, MA
GA-REL	——	Unkn-1992	No Mfg. HM	Providence, RI
GA-REL MFG. CO.	564 Manton Ave.	1992 -Present	——	Providence, RI
GARLAND ADVERTG.	149 Brunt St.	1992 -Present	——	Brooklyn, NY
GEMSCO INC.	395 4th Ave.	1930-1939	——	New York, NY
GEMSCO INC.	401 4th Ave.	1949-1968	——	New York, NY
GEMSCO INC.	——	1968-Present	Moved	Milford, CT
GEORGE F. CAKE CO.	——	1934-1978	By SUN & BLACKINTN	Berkeley, CA
GEO. F. HERALD CO.	7 Centre Mkt. Pl.	1920s	——	New York, NY
GEO. LAUTERER CO.	165 W. Madison	1937 & 39	——	Chicago, IL
GEO. J. MAYER CO.	142 S. Meridian	1939	——	Indianapolis, IN
GEO. P. KAUFMAN, PROP.	1511 Stout	1939	DENVER NOVELTY WKS	——
GEO. SCHENCK	——	1930-1966	SUN Buys in 1966	Los Angeles, CA

Hallmark Listing

Maker's Mark (as appears on badge)	Location	Year(s)	Additional	City/State
GERAGHTY & CO.	3036 W. Lake	1937 & 39	——	Chicago, IL
GERAGHTY INC, CHAS	1800 W. Roscoe	1949	——	Chicago, IL
GIBSON CO., A. C.	74 Oak St.	1937 & 39	——	Buffalo, NY
GIBSON CO., A. C.	Oak-Eagle Bldg	1949	——	Buffalo, NY
GOL-BEAM	——	Unkn.	By EVERSON-ROSS	NY & IL
GOLDBERG CO., PHILIP	70 Beach	1937	——	Boston, MA
GOLD PERMATONE	——	Unkn.	By ED JONES CO	Oakland, CA
GOPHER STAMP & DIE	——	1939	Badges	St. Paul, MN
GRAMMES	——	1915-1950s	See L.F.GRAMMES	Allentown, PA
GRAMMES & SONS, L.F.	239 Union St.	1937	——	Allentown, PA
GRAMMES & SONS, L.F.	398 Union St.	1944	——	Allentown, PA
GRAMMES & SONS, L.F.	380 Union St.	1949	——	Allentown, PA
G.R.D. CO.	Unkn.	Unkn.	U.S. Park Badges	——
GREENBLATT, CHARLES	——	Unkn.	Name HM	New York
GREEN COMPANY	1016 Walnut	1930-1949	——	Kansas City, MO
GREEN DUCK CO.	1721 W. North	1912-1948	——	Chicago, IL
GREEN DUCK CO.	Roscoe & Ravenwood	1949	Address HM, NLM	——
GREG G. WRIGHT & SON	CINITI,OHIO	1900-1930	City/State HM	Ohio
GREG WRIGHT & SONS	——	1930-1948	See WRIGHT & SONS	Cincinnati, OH
GREG WRIGHT-CINTI	——	1930-1970	Workhouse badges	Cincinnati, OH
GRIMM STAMP & BADGE	——	1910s	Badges	St. Louis, MO
GRIMM STAMP CO.	1314 Carr Ln.	1949	——	St. Louis, MO
GUS MESSING CO.	315 Jackson	1937 & 39	——	St. Paul, MN
GUS MESSING	——	Unkn.	See CARNES STAMP	St. Paul, MN
GUSTAVE FOX	——	1900-1950	See FOX-NLM	Cincinnati, OH
H.A. SLEEPER	——	1950s	St./City(abbr.)HM	Sacramento, CA
HAHN CO, IRVIN	Unkn.	1890-Unkn	——	Baltimore, MD
HAHN CO, IRVIN	207 Sharp	1937 & 39	2nd Add. Found	——
HAHN CO, IRVIN	1839 Worcester	1910s	1st a Add. Found	——
HAHN & CO.	——	1930-Present	See IRV. HAHN	Baltimore, MD
HAHN & CO.	207 Sharp	1937-Present	——	Baltimore, MD
HALTON MFG	——	Unkn.	TX Ranger Badges	Texas
HANEY CO., M.P.	813 "K" St. Sacto	1910s	CA Custom badges	——
HANSON, C.H.	305 W. Erie	1866-1987	——	Chicago, IL
HANSON, C.H.	303 W. Erie	1937	——	Chicago, IL
HANSON CO, THE C.H.	305 W. Erie	1949	——	Chicago, IL
HARCO INDUSTRIES	2362 Shangri-La	1992-Present	——	Phoenix, AZ
HARRIOT CO.	47 Winter	1937 & 49	——	Boston, MA
HARRIS CO. INC., BENJ.	229 Bowery	1937 & 49	——	New York, NY
HARRY BACHARACH NEW JERSEY (custom)	Unkn.	Jewelry Mfg.	New Jersey
HARRY C. BRADSHAW	93 Lafayette	1937 & 39	——	Newark, NJ
HARVEY & OTIS INC.	48 Chestnut	1937	——	Providence, RI
HARVEY & OTIS INC.	46 Chestnut	1939 & 49	——	Providence, RI
HARVEY SPOTRG., W.A.	Wash & Clinton	1949	——	Rochester, NY
HAMBURGER POLICE EQUIPMENT	Unkn.	1937	HM, Listed Co.	——
HAUSE, ROBERT L.	——	1898-1903	See ROULET	Toledo, OH
HAUSE & ROULET	——	1903-1911	Name Switches	Toledo, OH
HAUSMANN, INC.	——	1920-Unkn	Name HM	New Orleans, LA
H.C. LIEPSNER & CO MAKERS	K.C., MO.	1880-1920	City/State HM	——
H.C. LIEPSNER & CO.	938 Wyandotte	1920-1940	——	Kansas City, MO
H.C. MAGNUS & CO.	——	1890s	Name HM	——
HEADLEY ENGRAVING WKS.	4376 Ogden	1937 & 49	——	Chicago, IL

Hallmark Listing

Maker's Mark (as appears on badge)	Location	Year(s)	Additional	City/State
HEEREN BROS. & CO.	Pittsburgh, PA	Unkn.	Name HM	——
HELWIG & CO, LOUIS	205 W. Madison	1937	——	Chicago, IL
HELWIG & CO, WM.	434 Elm	1937 & 49	——	Cincinnati, OH
HELLENBUSH	Cincinnati, OH	1900-Unkn	Badges	——
HENRY MOSS & CO.	113-123 53rd	1922-1948	——	Brooklyn, NY
HENRY MOSS & CO.	115 53rd St.	1944	——	Brooklyn, NY
HENRY MOSS & CO.	——	1922-1938	Another Branch	Philadelphia, PA
HENDERSON AMES CO.	——	1950s	State Badges	Kalamazoo, MI
HEROLD, GEO.	7 Centre Mkt.	Unkn.		New York, NY
HICKOX-HIXSON BADGE	——	Unkn.	Unkn.	El Paso, TX
HI-GLO	——	1978-Present	BLACKINTON HM	Attleboro, MA
HISS COL'S	——	1922	HISS STAMP CO.	Columbus, OH
HISS-TOLEDO	——	1917-1922	Moved	Toledo, OH
H.L. SCHWARTZ & SONS MFG. CO.	——	1939	——	Benton Hbr., MI
H. MORTON & CO.	14th & Broadway	1915-1916	Custom Badges	——
H.M. NUTTER CO.	425 Montgomery St.	1924-1944	'18 Moise salesman	——
H.M. NUTTER CO.	Died '44, Wife operated	1944-1955	S. F. CAL., HM	San Francisco, CA
H.M. NUTTER CO.	S. F. CAL	1944-1955	To PATRICK in '55	San Francisco, CA
H.O. BATES	255 N Broad St.	1939	——	Elizabeth, NJ
HODGES BADGE CO.	166 Essex St.	1937 & 39	——	Boston, MA
HOOK-FAST	220 Eddy	1949	No Mfg. HM	Providence, RI
HOOK FAST SPECIALTS	63 Seymour St.	1992-Present	——	Providence, RI
H.R. TERRYBERRY	Grand Rapids	1939	Michigan	Grand Rapids, MI
H.T. COOK & CO.	——	1852-1887	Died, Co. Sold	Toledo, OH
HUEBEL MFG. CO.	103 Monroe	1937 & 49	——	Newark, NJ
HULSANDER ENG. CO.	Harris St.	1944 & 49	——	Trenton, NJ
HYATT MFG. CO.	1 N. Holiday	1937 & 39	——	Baltimore, MD
H.W. PETERS INC.	5178 Wash.	1939	——	Boston, MA
H.W. SCHWAB, INC.	43 Union Square	1939	——	New York, NY
I.B. & CO.	——	Unkn.	City HM	Philadelphia, PA
INDIANAPOLIS BADGE	3823 Mass. Ave.	1949-1991	IN, Address HM	——
INDIANAPOLIS BADGE	25 W. McLean Pl.	1992-Present	IN, Address HM	——
INGRAM-RICHARDSON MFG. CO. Oregon	1937		——	Beaver Falls, OR
INGRAM-RICHARDSON MF	1938 McMillan	1939	——	Beaver Falls, OR
IRVINE & WIRTH & J.	2439 Market	1906-1907	Temp/Earthquake	San Francisco, CA
IRVINE & WIRTH & J.	2129 Market	1907-1910	See J.C. IRVINE	San Francisco, CA
IRVINE & JACHENS	2129 Market	1909-1910	Wirth Died/New Co.	San Francisco, CA
IRVINE & JACHENS	1027 Market	1910-1925	Larger Bldg.	San Francisco, CA
IRVINE & JACHENS	1068 Mission	1926-1950	Address/City HM	San Francisco, CA
IRVINE & JACHENS	6700 Mission	1951-Present	Daly City, CA	San Francisco, CA
IRVIN HAHN CO.	Unkn. Starting Ad	1890-Unkn	——	Baltimore, MD
IRVIN HAHN CO.	207 Sharp	1937 & 39	——	Baltimore, MD
IRVIN H. HAHN CO	1830 Worcester	Unkn.-Present	——	Baltimore, MD
IRONS & RUSSELL CO.	——	1937 & 39	Listed Co.	Providence, RI
IRONS & RUSSELL CO.	95 Chestnut	1944	——	Providence, RI
IRWIN	——	Unkn.	Name HM	Portland, OR
IRWIN-HODSON CO.	——	1917-1970	City/State HM	Portland, OR
IRWIN-HODSON CO.	378 Washington St.	1895-1900	Badges perhaps	Portland, OR
IRWIN-HODSON CO.	401 Broadway	1930-1934	——	Portland, OR
IRWIN-HODSON CO.	439 N.W. 15th St.	1935-1970	——	Portland, OR
IRWIN-HODSON CO.	15th & Glisan	1937 & 49	——	Portland, OR
IVER JOHNSON CO.	——	1880-1900	City HM	Boston, MA

Hallmark Listing

Maker's Mark (as appears on badge)	Location	Year(s)	Additional	City/State
JACKSON HENRY	141 Fulton St.	1937	——	New York, NY
JACOB RABINOWITZ CO.	338 W. 37th St.	1949	——	New York, NY
JAMES & CO, ALLEN	——	1937	Listed Co.	Charleston, SC
JAS H MATTHEWS & CO	3942 Forbes St.	1890-1940s	——	Pittsburgh, PA
JAS H MATTHEWS & CO	2535 Forbes Fl	1937-1939	Listed Co.	Pittsburgh, PA
JAS. MURDOCK	——	1880-Unkn	Badges	Cincinnati, OH
J.B. CARROLL CO.	Albany & Carroll	1902-1950	——	Chicago, IL
J.C. DARLING CO.	——	1937 & 39	Listed Co.	Topeka, KS
J.C. IRVINE CO.	339 Kearney	1886-1896	General Engr.	San Francisco, CA
J.C. IRVINE CO.	343 Kearney	1896-1898	Founded, Bus. Add.	San Francisco, CA
J.C. IRVINE CO.	751 Market St.	1900-1906	Merged, IRVINE	San Francisco, CA
J. COOLEY MAKER	——	1939	Badges	Memphis, TN
J.C. DARLING	——	1939	Badges	Topeka, KS
JESSEL MARKING EQUIP	2207 Teall Ave.	1992-Present	——	Syracuse, NY
JENSENS (out of bus)	——	1930-Unkn	A.F. Jensen, jwlr	Omaha, NE
J.G. JOHNSTON CO.	——	Unkn	City HM	Boston, MA
J.H. FLEHARTY & CO.	——	Unkn	Old Co.	Cleveland, OH
J.K. NOVAK CO.	2703 Meyer Ave.	1949	——	Cleveland, OH
J.M.C. (pick & shovel)	——	1895-1932	See E.J. TOWLE	Seattle, WA
J.N. PHILLIPS CO.	——	1887-1890	627 J St.	Sacramento, CA
J.N. PHILLIPS CO.	1018 4th St.	1891-1897	——	Sacramento, CA
J.N. PHILLIPS CO.	627 D St.	1891-1913	Custom badges	——
J.N. PHILLIPS CO.	921 K St.	1913-1914	Sold to Haney	——
JOHN D MATTHEWS	——	1850-1890	Brass Stampings	Pittsburgh, PA
JOHN ROBBINS MFG. CO.	——	Unkn.	Moved	Boston, MA
JOHN ROBBINS MFG. CO.	23 Charles St.	1939	——	Cambridge, MA
JOHNSON CO, D. E.	164 W. 22nd St.	1937 & 39	——	New York, NY
JOHNSON & MEAHON	——	1880	City HM	Boston, MA
JOHNSON-NATIONAL INSIGNIA	——	1937 & 49	314 W. 14th St.	New York, NY
JOHNSON-NATIONAL INSIGNIA	RD 1	1992-Present	——	Cobleskill, NY
JOHNSON'S	1208 Brooklands	1992-Present	——	Dayton, OH
JOHNSTON BADGE	——	1887-Present	No Mfg. HM	Somerville, MA
JONAS BROTHERS	——	1910s	City HM	Dayton, OH
JONES EQUIPMENT CO.	——	1940-1977	Fl City Badges	Hollywood, FL
JOPLIN	——	Unkn.	See MERSON UNIFM	Joplin, MO
JOS. SAYRE	——	1866-1929	See SAYRE	Cincinnatti, OH
J.P. COOKE MFR'S	——	1903-1940	City HM	Omaha, NE
J.P. COOKE CO.	1309-15 Howard	1903-Present	——	Omaha, NE
J.P. COOKE CO.	——	1903-Present	City HM	Omaha, NE
J.P. COOKE OF OMAHA BY BLACKINTON		1983-Present	Cooke Dies	——
J.P. LOVELL & SONS	——	1880	City HM old badge	Boston, MA
J. RAUB CO.	——	Unkn.	City/State HM	New London, CT
J.R. GAUNT & SON	——	Unkn.	Made in England	Montreal, Canada
J. RITCHIE	——	1940s	Badges	New York, NY
JOS. SAYRE	——	1866-1929	See SAYRE below	Cinn, OH
J.S. PACKARD	206 Hudson	1937 & 39	——	New York, NY
J. & W. WHITE	——	Unkn.	City/State HM	Portland, OR
KAABLA	——	Unkn.	Out of business	Los Angeles, CA
KAAG TROPHIES	——	1946-1974	Sold SUN badge	Torrance, CA
KADUCK	Unkn.	Unkn.	Name HM	——
KARAT-CLAD	——	1978-Present	BLACKINTON HM	Attleboro, MA
KAUFMAN PROP., GEO P.	1511 Stout	1939	DENVER NVLTY. WKS.	Denver
KAUFMAN RUBBER STAMP	1511 Stout	1870-1945	——	Denver, CO
KAUTZ CO, FRED C.	2634 W. Lake	1937	——	Chicago, IL

Hallmark Listing

Maker's Mark (as appears on badge)	Location	Year(s)	Additional	City/State
KENNEDY NAME PLATE	4509 Pacific Bl.	1939-1949	——	Los Angeles, CA
KEYES-DAVIS CO.	18 Hanover St.	1944	Listed Co.	——
KEYSTONE BADGE CO.	——	1937 & 49	Listed Co.	Reading, PA
KEYSTONE BADGE CO.	806 Franklin	1992-Present	——	Reading, PA
KINNEY	——	1920s	City/State HM	Providence, RI
KIRK PLASTIC CO.	Jefferson & Maple	1949	——	Los Angeles, CA
KLINKNER & CO.	320 Sansome	1889-1898	See MOISE-KLINKNER	San Francisco, CA
KNICKERBOCKER STENCIL WORKS, NY	115 Nassau St.	1937	——	NY
KNIGHT TACTICS	316 S. Pickett	1992-Present	——	Alexandria, VA
KOEHLER STAMP & STE	406 W. Main St.	1920-1950s	——	Louisville, KY
KOEHLER STAMP & STE	406 W. Main St.	1949	Address HM	——
KOSTER CO., C.H.	79 Mercer, NYC	1937	Listed Co.	——
KRATZ CO.	1130 Clark St.	1939	——	Covington, KY
KRAUS & SONS INC.	157 Delancy	1937	——	New York, NY
KRAUS & SONS INC.	11 E. 22nd St.	1939 & 49	——	New York, NY
KREB BROTHERS	227 Washington St.	1911-1915	——	Portland, OR
KREB BROTHERS	112 2nd St., 2nd Fl.	1915-1917	——	Portland, OR
KREB BROTHERS	245 Stark St.	1917-1930	——	Portland, OR
KREB BROTHERS	267 Stark St.	1930-1935	Moved	Portland, OR
KREB BROTHERS	413 Stark St.	1935-1940	Moved	Portland, OR
KREB BROTHERS	82 & 204 S. W. Stark	1940-1957	Moved	Portland, OR
KREB BROTHERS	128 S. W. 3rd St.	1957-1958	Last Known Add	Portland, OR
KRENGEL MFG. CO.	229 Fulton	1949	——	New York, NY
LAMB SEAL & STENCIL	Wash., DC	1880-1890	Name/City/State HM	Wash., DC
LAMB SEAL CO.	Wash., DC	1890-1900	City/State HM	Wash., DC
LAMB & TILDEN	Wash., DC	1900-1916	New name	Wash., DC
LAMINEX INC.	——	1992-Present	Listed Co.	Charlotte, NC
LANE STAMP CO.	——	1939	Badges	San Diego, CA
LANG STAMP WKS.	Green & Drew	1939 & 49	——	Albany, NY
LANG STAMP CO.	18 Green St.	1992-Present	——	Albany, NY
LARSON & CO.	——	1920-1930	Name HM	San Francisco, CA
LARSON CO., C.W.	300 Ferry	1944	——	Pittsburgh, PA
LARSON CO., C.W.	Ferry & Larson	1949	——	Pittsburgh, PA
LARSCO	——	1890-1909	Early HM	Los Angeles, CA
LRSCO, MADE BY	——	1913-Unkn	Variation HM	Los Angeles, CA
LARSCO PRODUCT	——	Old Unkn.	City/State HM	Los Angeles, CA
LAS&SCO	——	Late 1930s	Variation HM	Los Angeles, CA
LAS & S CO.	——	Late 1930s	Variation HM	Los Angeles, CA
L. A. STAMP CO.	——	1884-1967	Another name	Los Angeles, CA
L. A. RUBBER STAMP	Temple & Spring	1884-1886	11 Allen Block	Los Angeles, CA
L. A. RUBBER STAMP	20-22 No. Spring	1886-1890	——	Los Angeles, CA
L. A. RUBBER STAMP CO.	123 No. Spring	1890-1891	Moved again	Los Angeles, CA
L. A. RUBBER STAMP CO.	224 W. First	1891-1910	Moved again	Los Angeles, CA
L. A. RUBBER STAMP	131 So. Spring	1910-1924	Inc.1915	Los Angeles, CA
L. A. RUBBER STAMP	1500 So. L. A.	1924-1935	New Location	Los Angeles, CA
L. A. STAMP & STATY. CO.	(acorn shape)	1935-1947	Variation HM	Los Angeles, CA
L. A. STAMP & STATY CO	(acorn shape)	1935-1947	No Periods HM	Los Angeles, CA
L. A. STAMP & STATY CO.	15th & L. A.	1949	——	Los Angeles, CA
L. A. STAMP & STATY	——	1935-1967	Out of business	Los Angeles, CA
LOS ANGELES RUB. STAMP CO.	(2 lines)	1880s	Early HM LASO#2	——
LAUTERER CO., GEO.	165 W. Madison	1937	——	Chicago, IL
L. BASCH & CO.	——	1907-1911	Badges	Toledo, OH

Hallmark Listing

Maker's Mark (as appears on badge)	Location	Year(s)	Additional	City/State
LAVIGNE, DONALD	——	Unkn.	City/State HM	Miami, FL
LEAVITT BROS.	5 Malden Ln.	1937 & 39	——	Attleboro, MA
L.F. GRAMMES & SONS	230 Union St.	1939	——	Allentown, PA
L.G. BALFOUR CO.	——	1939	Badges	Attleboro, MA
LEHMBERG & SONS, WM.	138 N. 10th St.	1937 & 39	——	Philadelphia, PA
LEHMBERG & SONS, WM.	141 N. 10th St.	1949	——	Philadelphia, PA
LEON FREEMAN	400 S. Wells	1930s	——	Chicago, IL
L.H. MOISE	320 Sansome	1893-1898	See MOISE-KLINKN	——
LIEPSNER & CO., H. C.	611 Delaware	1880-1913	——	Kansas City, MO
LIEPSNER & CO. MAKERS	(arch top)	1880-1920s	Actual HM	——
LIEPSNER & CO. H. C.	938 Delaware	1913-1921	Co. Listed Add	——
LIEPSNER & CO.	(Co. "o" in the C)	1927-Unkn	K.C.MO (in box)	——
LIEPSNER & CO.	208 W. 10th St.	1927-1937	Co. Listed Add	——
LIEPSNER & CO.	(straight two lines)	1930s	K.C.MO below	——
LIEPSNER & CO.	938 Wyandotte	1937-Present	——	Kansas City, MO
LIEPSNER & CO.	(fancy Sm.no city)	1940-Present	Variation HM	——
LIEPSNER & CO., H. C.	1513 Oak (mail)	1949-Present	K.C.,MO Listed	——
LILLEY-AMES CO.	——	1930-1939	Listed Co.	Columbus, OH
LIMERICK CO., J. ART.	202 W. Chase	1937	——	Baltimore, MD
LINCOLN STAMP & SEAL	——	1937 & 49	Badges	Lincoln, NE
LO-GLO	——	1978-Unkn	BLACKINTON HM	Attleboro, MA
LOUIS HELWIG & CO.	205 W. Madison	1939	——	Chicago, IL
LOUIS H. MARKOWITZ	136 Liberty	Late 1910s	——	NY City, NY
LOUIS MELIND CO.	362 W. Chicago	1937 & 39	——	Chicago, IL
L. SCHNEIDER	252 Market St.	1949	——	Newark, NJ
LOU-WALT INC.	821 Broadway	1937 & 49	——	New York, NY
LV/EY (in circle)	Unkn.	1939	LA Emerg/Council	——
LUCKE BADGE & BUTTON	1826 N. Fulton	1937 & 39	——	Baltimore, MD
LUCKE BADGE & BUTTON	1829 McKean	1949	——	Baltimore, MD
MACO	See Down "M"	Unkn.	One of the below	
M.A.G. (in oval)	——	1986-Present	AKA:METAL ARTS GRP	Seattle, WA
MANUFACTURERS SUPPLY CO.	72 Elm St.	1937 & 39	——	Providence, RI
MANUFACTURERS SUPPLY	174 Chesnut	1944 & 49	——	Providence, RI
MARSH MFG., CLEMENT J.	——	1937	Listed Co.	Scranton, PA
MARSH INC, CLEM	——	1949	Police & Fire	Scranton, PA
MARWYN CO.	Centre Mkt. Pl.	Unknown	N.Y.,NY HM	New York, NY
MATTHEWS & CO., JAS	——	1850-1890	Brass Stampings	Pittsburgh, PA
MATTHEWS & CO., JAS	3942 Forbes St.	1890-1939	——	Pittsburgh, PA
MATTHEWS & CO., JAS	2535 Forbes Fld	1939 & 49	——	Pittsburgh, PA
MAX MEYER	Unkn.	1890s	Hallmark	——
MAYER CO., GEO J.	142 S. Meridian	1937	——	Indianapolis, IN
MAYER CO., GEO. J.	17 N. Pennsylvania	1949	——	Indianapolis, IN
MAYER CO., G.J.	——	1960s	City (Abbr.)HM	Indianapolis, IN
MC INTOSCH, ROBERT	——	1867-1889	Badges	Toledo, OH
MCKINSTRY, SAM. K.	——	1871-1881	Died wife took Co.	Toledo, OH
MCKINSTRY MNF.JEWELER, ELLEN		1881-1885	Toledo Police	
M.E. CUNNINGHAM CO.	100 E. Carson	1937 & 39	——	Pittsburgh, PA
MEDALLIC ART CO.	210 51st St.	1939	——	New York, NY
MEDALLIC ART CO.	325 E. 45th St.	1949	——	New York,NY
MELIND, CO., LOUIS	362 W. Chicago	1937 & 39	——	Chicago, IL
MERCHANTS STAMP & STEN	182 W. Wash.	1937 & 39	——	Chicago, IL
MERCHANTS STAMP & STEN	186 W. Wash.	1949	——	Chicago, IL
MERKERT, NESS	61 Fulton St.	1937 & 39	——	New York, NY

Hallmark Listing

Maker's Mark (as appears on badge)	Location	Year(s)	Additional	City/State
MERKERT & SONS	70 Fulton St.	1949	——	New York, NY
MERSON	——	Unkn.	Variation HM	Joplin, MO
MERSON UNIFORM CO.	——	Unkn.	Name HM	Joplin, MO
MERSON UNIFORM CO.	——	Unkn.	City (Abbr.)HM	N. Y., NY
MESSING CO.	315 Jackson	1937 & 39	——	St. Paul, MN
METAL-ARTS	——	1930-33	LAPD Specials bldg.	Rochester, NY
METAL-ARTS CO.	Portland & Jackson Sts.	1939 & 49		Rochester, NY
MEYER & WENTHE	30 S. Jefferson	1900-1973	——	Chicago, IL
MEYER & WENTHE	30 S. Jefferson	1937 & 49	——	Chicago, IL
MEYER & WENTHE	——	1973-1985	Sold E.ROSS,NLM	Chicago, IL
MEYER INC., N. S.	419 49th Ave.	1937 & 39	——	New York, NY
MEYER INC., N. S.	4th & 29th St.	1949	——	New York, NY
MEYERS MILITARY SHOP	816 17th St.	1930	——	N. W. Wash. D. C.
MIDWEST	——	Unkn.	City (Abbr.)HM	Indianapolis, IN
MIDWEST FIRE & SAFETY CO.	——	1940s	City (Abbr.)HM	Indianapolis, IN
MINE SAFETY APPLS C	230 N. Braddock	1937 & 39	——	Pittsburgh, PA
MINNEAPOLIS STAMP & STENCIL CO.	——	1900s-Unkn	Badges HM	——
MITCHELL MFG. CO.	——	Old Unkn.	MA Forestry Badges	Boston, MA
MODERN STAMP MFG.	208 E. Baltimore	1937 & 49	——	Baltimore, MD
MOISE-KLINKNER CO.	320 Sansome	1898-1906	MOISE bought	San Francisco, CA
MOISE-KLINKNER CO.	417 Market	1906-1914	Moved	San Francisco, CA
MOISE-KLINKNER CO.	903 Fulton	1914-1919	Moved again	San Francisco, CA
MOISE-KLINKNER CO.	1212 Market	1919-1924	Moved again	San Francisco, CA
MOISE-KLINKNER CO.	309 Market	1924-1930	PATRICK Buys Co.	San Francisco, CA
MORSE & SON, C.H.	21 N Water St.	1939	——	Rochester, NY
MORSE & SON, C.H.	On Fee St.	1949	——	Rochester, NY
MORSE STAMP CO.	528 South Ave.	1992-Present	——	Rochester, NY
MORGAN JEWELRY CO.		1920s	S. F. badges	San Francisco, CA
MOSS AND CO.	Unkn. location	Unkn.	Variation	
MOSS CO., HENRY	113-123 53rd St.	1922-1938	——	Brooklyn, NY
MOSS & CO., HENRY	——	1922-1938	Another location	Philadelphia, PA
MOSS INC., SAMUEL H	40 E. 23rd St.	1949	——	New York, NY
MOSS CO., THEO.	35 Flatbush Ave.	1937 & 39	——	Brooklyn, NY
MUNICIPAL EQUIPMENT CO.	Scranton	1939	PA, listed Co.	PA
MURDOCK & SPENCER	139 W 5th St.	1866-1870	Address HM	——
MURDOCK, JAMES JR.	139 W 5th St.	1870-1876	Address HM	——
MURDOCK, JAMES JR.	165 Race St.	1876-1880	Address HM	——
MURDOCK, JAS.	(perhaps on Race St.)	1880	——	Cincinnati, OH
MURDOCK	165 Race St.	1880-1890	Address HM	——
MURDOCK, JR.,JAS.	52 Longworth	1890-1895	Variation HM	——
MURDOCK	52-60 Longworth	1895-1896	Address HM	——
MURDOCK	116-20 Longworth	1896-1905	Address HM	——
MURDOCK	116-20 Opera	1905-1910	Address HM	——
MURDOCK JR. CO, JAMES	"-120 Opera	1910-1915	Address HM	——
MURDOCK	——	1915-1919	Name HM	Cincinnati, OH
MURDOCK BUILDING	——	1919-1926	Bldg. HM	Cincinnati, OH
MURDOCK	125 W. Pearl	1926-1929	Address HM	
MURDOCK	——	1866-1931	Above dates	Cincinnati, OH
NAMECO BOSTON	——	1992-Present	New Listing	Somerville, MA
NATIONAL RUBBER STAMP CO., Toledo		1916	Badges	OH
NATIONAL STAMP & SEAL	250 Oak St.	1913-1924	——	Portland, OR
NATIONAL STAMP & SEAL	247 Washington	1924-1935	Badges	——
NATIONAL STAMP & SEAL	217 Washington	1935-1940	Out of Business	——

Hallmark Listing

Maker's Mark (as appears on badge)	Location	Year(s)	Additional	City/State
N.C. WALTER & CO.	5 Park Row	1870-1950s	Address HM	——
NELSON-SILVA	——	1970-1983	Name HM	Houston, TX
NESS & MERKERT	61 Fulton	1937 & 39	——	New York, NY
NEWARK EMBLEM	128 Market St.	1937	——	Newark, NJ
NEW YORK STENCIL WKS.	221 Fulton	1937 & 49	——	New York, NY
NEW YORK WOVEN LABEL MFG. CO NY NY	1937 & 39	36 W. 34th	New York, NY	
N.G. SLATER CORP.	3 W. 29th	1939	——	New York, NY
N.G. SLATER CORP.	7 W. 29th	1944-1949	——	New York, NY
NIELSON CO.	——	Unkn.	Name HM	New York, NY
NIELSEN-RIONDA, INC.	——	1952-1980	City HM,NLM	New York, NY
NIELSEN-RIONDA, INC.	——	1952-1971	See C. NIELSEN	New York, NY
NOACK CO.	——	Old unkn.	City/State HM	Detroit, MI
NOBLE & CHIPRON	224 W. First	1910-1942	AKA:CHIPRON	——
NOBLE & CO., F.H.	555 W. 59th	1937 & 39		Chicago, IL
NOBLE & WESTBROOK MFG. CO. "USA"	Old Unkn.	USA in 1860-1880	——	
NOBLE & WESTBROOK	19 Westbrook	1937 & 39	E. Hartford, CT	——
NOPD	(New Orleans PD shields)	Unkn-1986	See ED SMITH STEN	——
NORRIS STAMPING & MFG.	960 E. 61st	1935-1945	——	Los Angeles, CA
NORTHWESTERN STAMP WORKS	——	1888-1950	MN, City HM	St. Paul MN
N. STAFFORD CO.	131 N. 11th St.	1939	——	Brooklyn, NY
N. STAFFORD CO.	96 "R" Fulton St.	1939	——	New York, NY
N. STAFFORD CO.	96 Fulton, NY	1939	Nelson Stafford	NY
N. STAFFORD CO.	120 Fulton, NY	1949	See STAFFORD CO.	NY
NOVAK CO., J.K.	2703 Meyer Ave.	1949	——	Cleveland, OH
N. S. MEYER INC.	418 49th Ave.	1937-1949	——	New York, NY
N. S. MEYER INC.	4th & 29th St.	1949-1968	——	New York, NY
N. S. MEYER INC.	42 E. 20th St.	1968-Present	——	New York, NY
NY (current NYPD on-duty shield)	1990-Present	See SHERRY & "ES"	——	
O'BRIEN J. CO.	P.O. Box 221	1992-Present	——	Madison, NJ
OHIO STAMP & STENCIL CO,	1921	See CALDWELLS ——	Toledo, OH	
OK STAMP & SEAL	1608 Linwood	1899-Present	——	OK City, OK
OLD GLORY MFG. CO.	20 S. Wells	1937	——	Chicago, IL
OLD GLORY MFG. CO.	506 S. Wells	1939	——	Chicago, IL
OLD GLORY MFG. CO.	164 W Harrison	1949	——	Chicago, IL
OLYMPIC BADGE CO.	——	1920s	Badges w/ORBER	Providence, RI
ORANGE MFG. CORP.	61 Hoyt	1939	——	Newark, NJ
ORBER MFG. CO.	——	Unkn.-Present	Seldom HM	Garden, RI
OSBORNE COINAGE CO.	——	1947-1960	HM badges	Cincinnati, OH
OSBORNE REGISTER CO.	928 York St.	1939 & 49	——	Cincinnati, OH
PASQUALE SF. CAL	——	1912	City/St. (Abbr.)HM	San Francisco, CA
P.C. STAMP WKS.	——	1910s	AKA:PACIFIC COAST	Portland, OR
P.C. STAMP WKS.	——	1910-1950s	City HM Listed	Seattle, WA
P.C. STAMP WORKS	——	Unkn.	KREBS BROS.HM	Seattle, WA
PACIFIC COAST STAMP	2134 3rd Ave.	1944-1949	——	Seattle, WA
PACIFIC COAST STAMP WKS	207 Alder	1910-1915	——	Portland, OR
PACIFIC COAST STAMP WKS	231 Wash'n.	1915-1917	——	Portland, OR
PACIFIC COAST STAMP WKS	63 Broadway	1917-1922	Sold to KREBS BROS	——
PACIFIC COAST STAMP WKS	Unknown	1910-1922	——	Spokane, WA
PACIFIC RUBBER STAMP	——	1880-1926	1st screw press	Los Angeles, CA
PACKARD, J.S.	206 Hudson	1937 & 39	——	New York, NY
PANNIER	——	1910s	Badges	Pittsburgh, PA

Hallmark Listing

Maker's Mark (as appears on badge)	Location	Year(s)	Additional	City/State
PANNIER BROS STAMP CO	Sandusky No.	1937 & 39	———	Pittsburgh, PA
PANNIER CORP.	501 Pannier Bldg.	1944 & 49	———	Pittsburgh, PA
PARISIAN NOV. CO.	3502 S. Western	1895-1949	Badges	———
PARKER, T.M.	———	1880-Unkn	Hallmark	Hartford, CT
PARVA INDUSTRIES	2974 Whitney	1992-Present	———	Mt. Carmel, CT
PATRICK & CO.	310 California	1893-1894	———	San Francisco, CA
PATRICK & CO.	318 California	1894-1902	Moved	———
PATRICK & CO.	221 Sansome	1902-1903	Moved	———
PATRICK & CO.	111 Sansome	1903-1906	Earthquake	———
PATRICK & CO.	1534 Pine St.	1906-1907	Moved	———
PATRICK & CO.	126 Bush St.	1907-1908	Moved again	———
PATRICK & CO.	33 Sutter St.	1908	Moved again	———
PATRICK & CO.	1543 Pine St.	1906-1907	Moved	———
PATRICK & CO.	126 Bush St.	1907-1908	Moved again	———
PATRICK & CO.	33 Sutter St.	1908	Moved again	———
PATRICK & CO.	560 Market	1908-1963	Moved again	———
PATRICK MOISE-KLINKNER CO., CA	1930-1955	Bought MOISE-K.		———
PATRICK & CO.	561 Mission	1963-Unkn	70K SQ. FT. Bldg.	———
PATRICK & SONS	———	Unkn	See Above	San Francisco, CA
P & MK CO.	———	1930-1955	See Above	San Francisco, CA
PAT A PAD CO.	———	1939	Badges	Nashville, TN
P. DORMEY CO.	528 Walnut	1937 & 39	———	Cincinnati, OH
PEKROL TOOL CO.	2 Gt. Meadow Ln	1992-Present	———	E. Hanover, NJ
PETERS INC., H.W.	5178 Washington	1937	———	Boston, MA
PENFOLD MAKER	———	Unkn.	City/State HM	Buffalo, NY
PETTIBONE & CO	———	1904-1950s	City/State HM	Cincinnati, OH
PETTIBONE BROS. MFG. CO.	626 Main	1870-1939	———	Cincinnati, OH
PETTIBONE BROS. MFG.	628 Sycamore	1944 & 49	———	Cincinnati, OH
PETTIBONE-CINTI.	———	1920s	Name/City (Abbr.)	Cincinnati, OH
PHILADELPHIA BADGE CO	940 Market	1900-1950s	———	Philadelphia, PA
PHILADELPHIA BADGE CO	1005 Filbert	1944	———	Philadelphia, PA
PHILADELPHIA BADGE CO	1007 Filbert	1949-1950s	———	Philadelphia, PA
PHILIP GOLDBERG CO.	70 Beach	1939	———	Boston, MA
PHILIPS POLICE EQU.	316 S. Pickett	1992-Present	———	Alexandria, VA
PHILLIPS MFG. CO.	190 Emmett	1939	———	Newark, NJ
PIN KING OF AMERICA	7250 Harwin	1992-Present	———	Houston, TX
PIN WORKS	432 Mill St.	1992-Present	———	Long Lake, MN
PIONEER RUBBER STAMP	———	1900s	Name HM	Des Moines, IA
PIONEER	705 BDWY. OAKLAND	1920s	City/Street HM	———
PILGRIM BADGE & LABEL	612 Memorial	1937	———	Cambridge, MA
PILGRIM BADGE & LABEL	609 Memorial	1939	———	Cambridge, MA
PILRGIM BADGE & SPLTY	216 Vassar S	1944	———	Cambridge, MA
PILGRIM BADGE & SPEC.	292 Babcock	1949-1950s	Boston 15, MA	Boston, MA
PITT PRODUCTS INC.	197 Sussex Ave	1949	———	Newark, NJ
PLATILOY	———	1939-Present	ENTENMANN HM	Los Angeles, CA
P. NANNOLA	7 Centre Mkt Pl	Unkn	HM- N.Y.NY	New York, NY
P.N.P. LTD. VANCOUVER,B.C.	———	1920s	Badges	Canada
POPULAR EMB. & MEDAL	180 Fulton	1949		New York, NY
PORTLAND STAMP & SEAL WORKS	———	1924-1980	Full name	———
PORTLAND STAMP & S.	163 1st St.	1924-1930	Founded by 2	———
PORTLAND STAMP & S.	83 5th Ave.	1930-1935	———	Portland, OR

Hallmark Listing

Maker's Mark (as appears on badge)	Location	Year(s)	Additional	City/State
PORTLAND STAMP & S.	512 S.W. Oak	1935-1950	——	Portland, OR
PORTLAND STAMP & S.	513 S.W. Pine	1950-1970	Moved	Portland, OR
PORTLAND STAMP & S.	128 S.W. 3rd	1970-Present	Current Add.	Portland, OR
POTTER, L.A.	——	1916	Badges	Toledo, OH
POWER CO, R.B.	——	1939	Badges	Ashley, OH
PRICING PRESS	105 Lafayette	1949-1950s	NY 13,NY	New York, NY
P. SLEEPER CO.	——	1940-1950	See SLEEPER	Sacramento, CA
PUDLIN CO., M.	286 5th Ave.	1949	——	New York, NY
PUGET SOUND BADGE WKS.	——	Unkn.	Name HM	WA
PYRAMID STAMP & TOOL	2000 Porter	1931-1950s	——	Detroit, MI
QUERL & COLEMAN	——	1911	Badges	Toledo, OH
QUINTS SONS CO, S.H.	15 S. 4th St.	1937	——	Philadelphia, PA
QUINTS SONS CO, S.H.	4th & Holden	1939	——	Philadelphia, PA
QUINTS SONS CO, S.H.	13 S. 4th St.	1949	——	Philadelphia, PA
RABIPresentITZ CO, JACOB	338 W 37th St.	1949	——	New York, NY
R.B. POWER CO.	——	1939	Badges	Ashley, OH
REESE, CHAS. D.	57 Warren	1930s-1939	Name HM	NYC, NY
REESE, C.D.	67 Warren	Unkn.	Add/City HM	NYC, NY
REESE, C.D.	57 Warren	1930-1939	Add/City HM	NYC, NY
REESE, CO.	57 Warren	1930-Present	See C.D. & S.H.	NYC, NY
REESE CO., STANLEY	57 Warren	1937 & 49	Listed Co.	NYC, NY
REESE, S.H.	57 Warren,	1939-Present	Add/City/State HM	NYC, NY
REILLY	15 Cornhill	1880	City HM	Boston, MA
REININGER & LARREMAN	749 Market	1906-1908	——	San Francisco, CA
REININGER, AUGUST CO	4652 18th St.	1908-1910	Custom badges	San Francisco, CA
REININGER & CO SF CAL	541 Market	1910-1914	City/State HM	San Francisco, CA
REININGER & CO SF CAL	420 Market	1915-1931	City/State HM	San Francisco, CA
RESKREM SILVER MFG.	872 Broadway	1937 & 39	——	New York, NY
RESKREM SILVER MFG.	76 Forsyth	1949	——	New York, NY
RIKER BROS.	46 Court	1937	——	Newark, NJ
ROBERT STROLL	70 Fulton	1939	——	New York, NY
ROBBINS, CHARLES	In Res. Garage	1892-1910	First Home Bus.	——
ROBBINS CO, THE	100 Hazelschool	1896-1916	——	Attleboro, MA
ROBBINS CO./METAL	Unkn	1941-1970	Name HM	——
ROBBINS CO., THE	100 Hazelschool	1937 & 49	——	Attleboro, MA
ROBBINS MFG. CO, JOHN	23 Charles	1937	——	Cambridge, MA
ROBBINS MFG. CO. JOHN	71 Hampshire	1949	——	Cambridge, MA
ROD A. BACHELDER	——	1890s	Badges	Portland, ME
ROULET	——	1880	Badges	Toledo, OH
ROULET & ARMSTRONG	——	1881-1897	Name HM	Toledo, OH
ROULET & CO.	——	1897-1898	See HAUSE & R.	Toledo, OH
ROULET & HAUSE	——	1903-1911	Badges	Toledo, OH
ROULET & SON	——	1911-1915	Name HM	Toledo, OH
THE ROULET CO.	——	1915-1979	Started 1881	Toledo, OH
RHO-GLO	——	1978-Present	BLACKINTON HM	Attleboro, MA
ROBBERSON STEEL CO.	McKinley & 3rd	1949	——	OK City, OK
ROYAL INCENTIVES	43 John St.	1944	——	New York, NY
R-S-T CO.	——	1949	City/St. (Abbr.) HM	Kan. City, KA
RUSSELL-HAMPTON CO.	325 W. Madison	1937 & 39	——	Chicago, IL
RUSSELL UNIFORM CO.	194 Lexington	1949-1959	N.Y.16, NY HM	New York, NY
RUSSELL UNIFORM CO.	42 E. 20th St.	1992-Present	——	New York, NY
RUSSELL UNIFORM CO.	NEW YORK	——	1930s-Unkn	City HM
SABATINI		Unkn.	Jeweler in SF	San Francisco, CA
SACKMAN STAMP & STENCIL CO.	Unkn.	1939	——	Akron, OH

Hallmark Listing

Maker's Mark (as appears on badge)	Location	Year(s)	Additional	City/State
SACKMAN STAMP & STE	80 W. Exchange	1944	——	Akron, OH
SACKMAN STAMP & STE 76 W. Exchange		1949	——	Akron, OH
S.A. FRENCH CO.	——	1887-1926	Out of Business	New York, NY
SACHS LAWLOR	——	1881-Present	Since 1977 NLM	Denver, CO
SACHS-LAWLOR CO. MAKERS	——	1949	City HM	Denver, CO
SACHS LAWLOR M & M DENVER,COLO.	——		Unkn.	City/State HM
SALCO	——	1881-1965	SACHS LAWLOR H	——
SALT LAKE STAMP CO.	——	1939	Listed Co. 1939	Salt Lake City, UT
SALT LAKE STAMP	——	1910-1968	Badges	UT
SALT LAKE STAMO CO.	41 W. 3rd So. St.	1944 & 49	Name HM	UT
SAMUEL F. CURRY	44 N. 4th St.	1937 & 39	——	Philadelphia, PA
SAMUEL CURRY INC.	231 Chestnut	1949	——	Philadelphia, PA
SAMUELS & CO. JEWELERS	——	1930s	City (Abbr.) HM	San Francisco, CA
SAMUELS CO, ALBERT	——	1920-1930s	Jeweler HM	San Francisco, CA
SANDERS MFG. CO.	Sanders Block	1937 & 49	——	Nashville, TN
SAYRE, JOS. J.	137 Mound St.	1866-1867	——	Cincinnati, OH
SAYRE, JOS. J.	4th & Walnut Sts	1867-1877	Address HM	Cincinnati, OH
SAYRE, JOS. J.	36 W. 4th St.	1877-1890	Address HM	Cincinnati, OH
SAYRE	36 W. 4th St.	1890-1895	Address HM	Cincinnati, OH
SAYRE & SON, JOS. J. CIN.O. (Abbr.)	——	Unkn.	City/State HM	Cincinnati, OH
SAYRE & SON, JOS.	112 E. 4th St.	1895-1896	Address HM	Cincinnati, OH
SAYRE & SON	114 E. 4th St.	1896-1900	Address HM	Cincinnati, OH
SAYRE & SON, JOS.	110-114 E. 4th	1900-1905	Address HM	Cincinnati, OH
SAYRE & SON, JOS.	110 E. 4th St.	1905-1910	Address HM	Cincinnati, OH
SAYRE & SON	220 E. 6th St.	1910-1915	Address HM	Cincinnati, OH
SAYRE	220 E. 6th St.	1915-1919	Address HM	Cincinnati, OH
SAYRE	417 Main St.	1919-1929	HM & stencils	Cincinnati, OH
SCHLECHTER, EDW. H.	——	1937 & 49	Listed Co.	Allentown, PA
SCHNEIDER, L.	252 Market	1949	——	Newark, NJ
SCHWAAB S & S CO.	——	Unkn.	City HM	Milwaukee, WI
SCHWAAB STAMP & SEA	545 N Water St.	1937 & 49	——	Milwaukee, WI
SCHWAAB INC.	11415 W. Burleigh	1992-Present	——	Milwaukee, WI
SCHWAB, H. W. & I., INC.	43 Union Sq.	1939 & 49	——	New York, NY
SCHWARTZ KIRWIN & FAUSS	53 Park Pl	1937 & 39	——	New York, NY
SCHWEIZER CO.	223-229 Russell	1939 & 49	——	St. Louis, MO
SCHWEIZER CO, CHAS.	223-29 Russell	1939	——	St. Louis, MO
SCHWERDTLE STAMP CO.	9 Cannon St.	1935-1941	——	Bridgeport, CT
SCHWERDTLE STAMP CO.	152 Elm St.	1944	Listed Co.	——
SCHWERDTLE STAMP CO.	1069 Elm St.	1949	Listed Co.	——
SCHWERDTLE STAMP CO.	168 Elm St.	1992-Present	——	Bridgeport, CT
SCOVILL MFG. CO.	75 Mill St.	1939	——	Waterbury, CT
SCOVILL MFG. CO.	100 Mill St.	1949	——	Waterbury, CT
S. D. CHILDS	——	1850-1940s	Badges	Chicago, IL
S. D. CHILDS & CO.	17 No Loomis	1937 & 39	——	Chicago, IL
S. D. CHILDS JR. & CO.	17 No Loomis	1939	——	Chicago, IL
S. D. CHILDS CO.	——	1910-Unkn	Another Branch	Toledo, OH
SEATTLE RUBBER STAMP	——	Unkn.	Badges	Seattle, WA
S. E. EBY CO.	——	1935-Unkn	Name HM	Philadelphia, PA
SEIDERS CO, SETH	——	1910	Badges	Toledo, OH
SENTIS STENCIL WKS.	41-43 Park Pl.	1949	——	New York, NY
S.G. ADAMS CO.	411 N. 6th	1939	——	St. Louis, MO
S.G. ADAMS CO.	414 Lucas Ave.	1949-1950s	Address HM	St. Louis, MO
S.G. ADAMS S&S CO.	——	1893-1934	Badges	St. Louis, MO

Hallmark Listing

Maker's Mark (as appears on badge)	Location	Year(s)	Additional	City/State
SHAW CO, E. C.	312 Main St.	1937 & 49	——	Cincinnati, OH
SHERRY	15 Eldridge	1962-Present	See ES & NY	N.Y.,NY
SHERMAN MFG. CO.	74 Clifford St.	1937 & 49	——	Providence, RI
S.H. QUINTS SONS CO.	4th & Holden	1939	——	Philadelphia, PA
S.H. REESE	57 Warren St.	1939-Present	See C.D. Reese	NYC, NY
SHIELD RESEARCH	Unkn.	Unkn.	Hallmark	——
SHREVE AND CO.	——	1930-Unkn	Solid Gold SF Badges	San Francisco, CA
S.H. STRAUB MAKER	——	Late 1900	City/State HM	Kalamazoo, MI
SIMON INC., E. & H.	381 4th Ave.	1949	——	New York, NY
SIMMANGS	——	1887-Unkn	Name HM	San Antonio TX
SIMMONS, ST. LOUIS MO/KS (both)	——	1880-Unkn	US Marshal's Bldge.	——
SIMMANGS	——	1887-Unkn	Name HM	——
SLEEPER	825 "J" St.	1940-1950	——	Sacramento, CA
SLEEPER SAC'TO, CAL	——	1950s	City/State HM	Sacramento, CA
SLEEPER CO., P.	——	1940-1950	City/State HM	Sacramento, CA
SMITH ED. STENCIL WKS	416 Camp St.	1937	——	New Orleans, LA
SMITH & WARREN CO.	72 Fulton	1949-1970	N.Y.,NY City HM	NY
SMITH & WARREN	127 Oakley Ave.	Present	——	White Plains, NY
S.M. SPENCER MFG.	——	1920-1960	Out of Business	Boston, MA
S.M. SPENCER MFG. CO.	3 Cornhill	1937 & 49	——	Boston, MA
SOME'S UNIFORMS INC.	63 Rte N. 17	1992-Present	——	Paramus, NJ
SOMMER BADGE MFG. CO.	71 Liberty	1937 & 49	——	Newark, NJ
SOUTHARD CALENDAR & PRINTING CO.	——	1939	——	Columbus, OH
SOUTH BADGE	——	Unkn.	Badge HM	——
SO. BROOKLYN RUBBER STAMP	569 6th	1992-Present	——	Brooklyn, NY
SOUTHERLAND STAMP CO	——	1949	Listed Co.	San Diego, CA
SOUTHERN STAMP & STATIONARY CO.		1937 & 39	——	Richmond, VA
SOUTHERN STAMP & STATY	13th & Main	1949	——	Richmond,VA
SOUTHWESTERN STAMP WORKS	——	1930-1962	Name HM	OK City, OK
SOUTHWESTERN STAMPS	——	1963-Unkn	Name Change	OK City, OK
SPEIS BROS.	27 E. Monroe	1937 & 39	——	Chicago, IL
SPENCER, WM.	153 W 5th St.	1870-1877	——	Cincinnati, OH
SPENCER	153 W 5th St.	1877-Unkn	——	Cincinnati, OH
SPENCER MFG CO, S.M.	3 Cornhill	1937 &49	Boston, MASS HM	Boston, MA
SPOKANE STAMP WKS.	——	1883-Present	HM to 1938, NLM	Spokane, WA
STAATS & CO., E.G.	——	1937 & 49	Listed Co.	Mt. Pleasant, IA
STAFFORD CO.	96 "R" Fulton	1937	See N. STAFFORD	NY
STANDARD EMBLEM CO.	184 Wash.	1937	——	Providence, RI
STANDARD EMBLEM CO.	53 Clifford St.	1939	——	Providence, RI
STANDARD EMBLEM CO.	7 Beverly	1944 & 49	——	Providence, RI
STAR ENG.	——	Unkn.	Name HM	Houston, TX
STAR PRINTING CO.	——	1851-1865	LAPD Ribbon badge	East L.A., CA
STECKLER	——	Unkn-1970s	L.A.S.O. pins	New York
STEINER E & B CO.	——	Unkn.	City HM	St. Louis, MO
STEINER ENGRAVING & BDGE	——	1937 & 39	2000 Mulanphy St.	St. Louis, MO
STEINER S. S. CO.	——	1900-Unkn	Mid-west Co.	St. Louis, MO
STEWART & CO.	82 Duane St.	1937	——	New York, NY
STEWART & CO, R.A.	80 Duane St.	1939	——	New York, NY
STEWART & CO, R.A.	89 Duane St.	1949	——	New York, NY
STOEFFELS SEALS	——	Unkn.	Plastic badges	New York, NY
ST. LOUIS BUTTON & MFG.	414 Lucas	1893-1950s	——	St. Louis, MO

Hallmark Listing

Maker's Mark (as appears on badge)	Location	Year(s)	Additional	City/State
ST. PAUL STAMP WKS.	65 E 5th	1920-1950s	——	St. Paul, MN
STROLL, ROBERT	70 Fulton	1937 & 39	——	New York, NY
SUN BADGE L. A.	——	1958-1974	Buys GEO.SCHENCK	Los Angeles, CA
SUN BADGE CO. L. A. CO.	712 W. Cienega	1974-Present	——	San Dimas, CA
SUPERIOR SEAL & STAMP	1400 Vermont	1909-1949	——	Detroit, MI
SUPERIOR STAMP CO.	——	1897-1916	See BOARDMAN	Toledo, OH
TACOMA RUBBER STAMP CO.	——	1940s	City/State HM	Tacoma, WA
TAYLOR BROS. CO.	700 W. Superior Ave.	1937 & 39	——	Cleveland, OH
TAYLOR BROS. CO. MFRS.	CLEVELAND,O.			
	——	1930s	City/State HM	Cleveland, OH
THEO. MOSS CO.	35 Flatbush	1939	——	Brooklyn, NY
THREE RIVERS REFINING	1506 Wall	1992-Present	——	Ft. Wayne, IN
TIFFANY & CO.	——	1900-Unkn	Jewelry Co. HM	New York, NY
TINSEL TRADING CO.	9 W. 36th St.	1949	——	New York, NY
TIPP NOVELTY CO.	Tippecanoe City	1937 & 39	Ohio Co.	OH
T.M. PARKER	——	1880-Unkn	City/State HM	Hartford, Conn.
TOLEDO RUBBER STAMP CO.	——	1884-1892	First Name HM	Toledo, OH
TOLEDO STAMP & STENCIL WORKS, OH	——	1892-1922	Next HM	——
TOLEDO STAMP & STENCIL CO.	Toledo	1922-Present	Badges	Toledo, OH
TOLEDO STAMP & STENCIL	——	1937 & 49	Listed Co.	Toledo, OH
TORSCH & FRANZ BADGE	3 N. Liberty	1937 & 49	——	Baltimore, MD
TOWEER & LYON	85 Chambers	Unkn-1889	No Longer Mfg.	NY
TOWLE, E.J.	——	1930s	HM State	Seattle, WA
TOWLE CO, E.J.	——	1930s	HM State	Seattle, WA
TWIN CITY STAMP & STEN	306 3rd Ave.	1937 & 39	——	Minneapolis, MN
TWIN CITY STAMP & STE	516 S 5th St.	1949	——	Minn., MN
UHL BROS. CO.	——	1899-1903	Badges	Toledo, OH
UNION LABEL	——	1930s-1956	Early IRVINE & J	San Francisco, CA
UNITED INSIGNIA	——	Unkn.	Badges	New York, NY
UNITED UNIFORM CO.	——	Unkn.	Badges	Buffalo, NY
U.S. BADGE CO. LTD.	——	Unkn.	Badges	Staten Is., NY
UTAH STAMP CO.	——	1939	Badges	Utah
V & V MFG.	15330 Proctor, Industry	1980-Present	badges	CA
V.H. BLACKINTON MA	——	1860-Present	HMs 1st in 1978	Attleboro Falls,
V.H. BLACKINTON	221 John Dietsch	1992-Present	Blvd., MA	MA
W. & H. CO.	——	1917-Unkn	City/State HM	Newark, NJ
WALTCO INC.	30 E. 4th St.	1949	——	New York, NY
WALTER & SONS, N. C.	5 Park Row	1870-1950s	——	New York, NY
WARD STILLISON CO.	——	1937 & 39	Badges	Anderson, IN
WARNER WOVEN LABEL CO.	——	1939	Badges	Paterson, NJ
WATERBURY BUTTON & MFG.	——	1937 & 39	CT, Badges	Waterbury, CT
WATERBURY COMPANIES	Production Rd.	1949	——	Waterbury, CT
W & A (WMS & ANDERSON)	——	1930s-Present	Ref. CHP Badges	Providence, RI
WATKINS R. METALCRFT	2253 E. 75th	1949	——	Chicago, IL
WCO	HM Unkn.	Unkn.	Gold US MRSHL'S	——
W.E. (pick & shovel)	——	1981-1986	Change See M.A.G.	Seattle, WA
WENDELL & CO.	55 E. Washington	1937 & 49	——	Chicago, IL
WENDELL'S INC.	——	1940s	Badges	Minneapolis, MN
WENDELL'S INC.	325 Marquette	1937-1940s	——	Minneapolis, MN
WENDELL-NORTHWESTERN	——	1950s	MN, Merged Co.	Minneapolis, MN
WESTERN BADGE & STAMP	——	1951-1959	Badges	St. Paul, MN

Hallmark Listing

Maker's Mark (as appears on badge)	Location	Year(s)	Additional	City/State
WESTERN BADGE & NOV	402 N Exchange	1937 & 49	——	St. Paul, MN
WESTERN STAMP	——	1880-1950	Name HM, NLM	Omaha, NE
WESTERN STAMP & STEN.	1120 Farham	1937 & 39	HM Variation	——
WEYHING	——	1930-Present	City HM	Detroit, MI
WEYHING BROS.	——	Unkn.-Present	City HM	Detroit, MI
WEYHING BROS. MFG.	302 Eaton Tower	1937 & 39	——	Detroit, MI
WEYHING BROS. MFG D	Broderick Tower	1949	——	Detroit, MI
W. F. STEPHENS JR INC.	——	Unkn.	City/State HM	Franklin, OH
WHITEHEAD & HOAG CO.	105 First St.	1910-1954	——	Newark, NJ
WHITEHEAD & HOAG CO.	——	1901-1930	Toledo Branch	Toledo, OH
WHITE J. & W.	——	Unkn.	Badges	Portland, OR
WILCOX CO, W. W.	——	1920s	City HM	Chicago, IL
WILCOX MFG CO, W. W.	564 W. Randolph	1937 & 49	——	Chicago, IL
WILKES-BARRE REGALIA FACTORY Unkn.		1937 & 39	——	Pennsylvania
WILLIAMSON STAMP CO.	16 No. Third	1930-1950	——	Minneapolis, MN
WILLIAMS & ANDERSON CO.	14 3rd St.	1937 & 49	——	Providence, RI
WILLIAMS & ANDERSON	——	1930s-Present	See W & A	Providence, RI
WILL & FINCK MAKERS S.F.,CA	——	1910-1930	Badges	
W.D. COOLEY	——	Unkn.	Name HM	Memphis, TN
W.J. COOLEY & CO.	Fernando & Gayoso	1939	——	Memphis, TN
W.J. COOLEY & CO.	102 Hernando	1944 & 49	——	Memphis, TN
WM. A. FORCE CO.	222 Nichols Ave.	1949	——	Brooklyn, NY
WM. HELWIG & CO.	434 Elm, Cinn.	1939	OH, Listed Co.	Cincinnati, OH
WM. LEHMBERG & SONS	138 N. 10th St.	1937 & 39	——	Philadelphia, PA
WM. LEHMBERG & SONS	141 N. 10th St.	1949	——	Philadelphia, PA
WM. SCHRIDDLE CO.	107 N. Wacker	1939	——	Chicago, IL
W.S. CO. M.P.L.S.	——	1940s	Badges	Minneapolis, MN
W. SCULLY	Unkn.	Unkn.	Name HM	
W.S. DARLEY & CO.	2812 W. Washington	1943-1963	——	Chicago, IL
W.S. DARLEY & CO.	——	Unkn.	City/State HM	Melrose Park, IL
W.S. DARLEY	——	Unkn.	Variation	Melrose Park, IL
W.S. DARLEY & CO.	Chicago 12	Unkn.	HM B-4 Zip Codes	
WIRTH & JACHENS	339 Kearney	1900-1906	See IRVINE, WIRTH	San Francisco, CA
WRIGHT & DENISON	136 W. 4th St.	1867-1877	——	Cincinnati, OH
WRIGHT & SONS	——	Unkn.	Left DENISON	Cincinnati, OH
WRIGHT, GREG G.	167 Race St.	1877-1890	Address HM	——
WRIGHT & SON, GREG	50 Longworth	1890-1896	Address HM	——
WRIGHT & SON, GREG G. CINITI,OHIO	——	1900-1930	City/State HM	——
WRIGHT & SON, GREG	112 Longworth	1896-1905	Address HM	——
WRIGHT	112-114 Opera	1905-1910	Address HM	——
WRIGHT & SON, GREG	117 Opera Pl.	1910-1915	Address HM	——
WRIGHT-CINTI., GREG	Unkn.	1930-1970	HM Workhouse badges	——
WRIGHT	119 Opera Pl.	1915-1927	Address HM	——
WRIGHT	——	1928-1929	Name HM	Cincinnati, OH
WRIGHT	119 Opera Pl.	1930-1936	Address HM	——
WRIGHT & SONS, GREG	121 Opera Pl.	1937 & 49	——	Cincinnati, OH
WRIGHT & SONS, GREG W.	8th Street	1970s	——	Cincinnati, OH
WRIGHT CO, KAY	1500 Woodward Ave.	1937 & 39	——	Detroit, MI
W. W. WILCOX CO.	——	1920s	City HM	Chicago, IL
W. W. WILCOX MFG. CO	564 W. Randolph	1939	——	Chicago, IL

"Best Stamp K.C. MO."

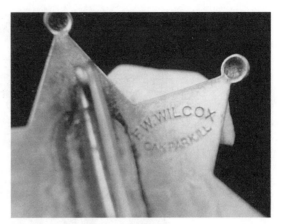

"F.W. Wilcox Oak Park, Ill."

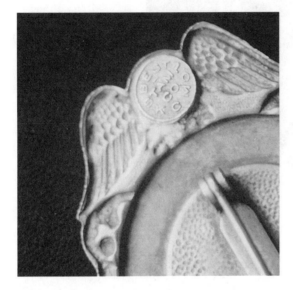

"Best Stamp Co. KC MO" Medallion hallmark.

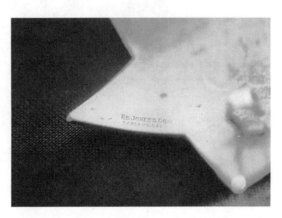

"Ed Jones & Co. Oakland, Cal."

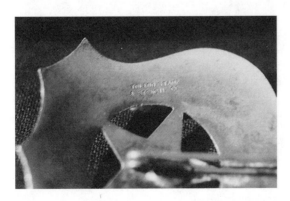

"Toledo Stamp & Stencil Co."

"Los Angeles Rubber Stamp Co." Pre-1935 hallmark.

49

Ornate, gold-plated eagle-top shield with owner's name marked on back, "H.A. Anderson."

"Sun Badge Co. San Dimas, CA, Made in USA."

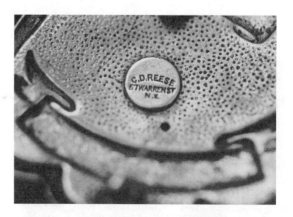

"C.D. Reese 57 Warren St. N.Y." 1930-1939 medallion hallmark.

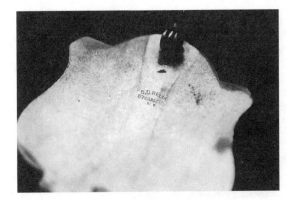

"C.D. Reese 57 Warren St. N.Y." Stamped hallmark.

"W.J. Cooley Maker Memphis, Tenn."

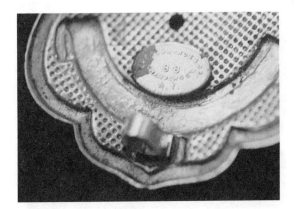

"Everson-Ross Co. 88 Chambers St. N.Y." 1905-1950 hallmark.

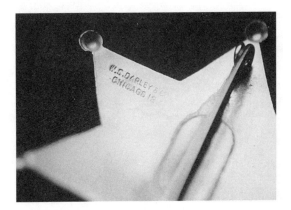

"W.S. Darley & Co. Chicago 12."

"Art Burnside Police Equipment Spokane, Wash."

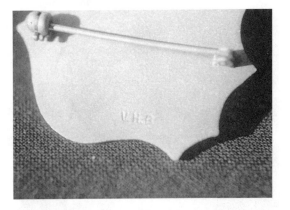

"V.H.B." Modern hallmark of V.H. Blackinton & Co.

"BLACKINTON" modern script style hallmark.

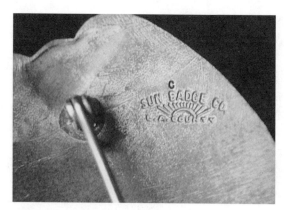

"Sun Badge Co. LA County."

"Entenmann-Rovin Co. Genuine "Carltone Gold'
Pico Rivera, Calif."

"Irvine & Jachens S.F."

"George F. Cake Co. Berkeley, Cal."

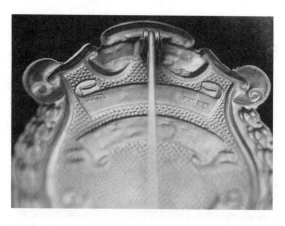

"LAS & SCO Nickel Silver" Late 1930s hallmark.

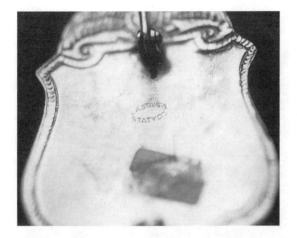

"L.A. Stamp & Staty Co." 1935-1947 hallmark.

"BNB Phoenix AZ."

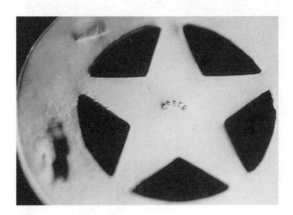

"Orber" Rhode Island Co.

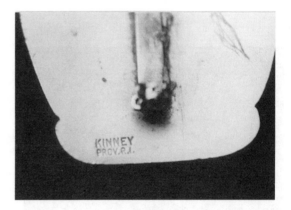

"Kinney Prov. R.I." 1920s hallmark.

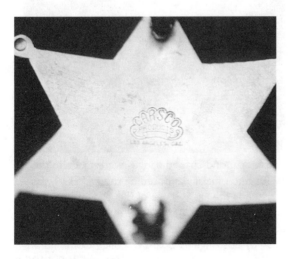

"Larsco Products Los Angeles, Cal."

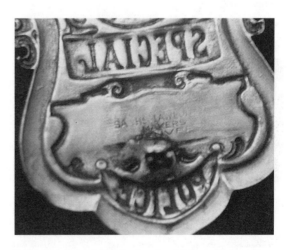

Difficult to read, "Sachs-Lawlor Makers Denver" 1920s hallmark.

"The Whitehead & Hoag Co. Newark, N.J." 1910-1954 hallmark (1940s badge).

"Greg G. Wright & Sons Badges Cincinnati, O." A fairly rare Los Angeles Police badge, known as the Series 5-1/2.

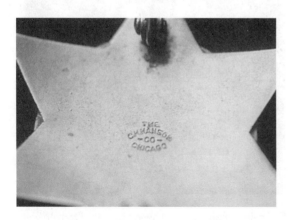

"The C.H. Hanson CO. Chicago." 1940s-1950s hallmark.

These diamond-shaped badges were made in the 1920s, and officially adopted by the LAPD. Mystery surrounds the life and use of this badge. Badge number (on front) and control number (on back) do not match. Hallmark reads, "2491 Copyright 1930 by Los Angeles Board of Police Commissioners." **Value: $300-$400**

"S.H. Reese 57 Warren St. New York, N.Y." 1939 to present hallmark.

"Pacific Emblem Seattle, Wash." Circa 1935.

"J.P. Cooke Co. Mfr's Omaha."

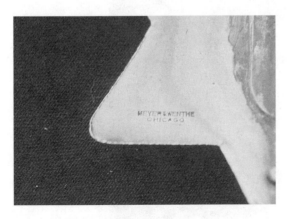

"Meyer & Wenthe Chicago."

"Smith & Warren."

"Blackinton" script with:"24kt Karatclad HCE."

"Govt. Property C.W. Nielsen Mfg."

"S.M. Spencer Mfg. Co. Boston."

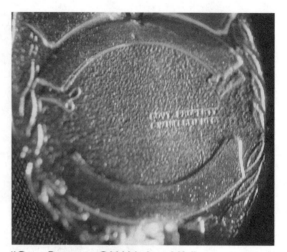

"The Ed Jones Co. Oakland, Cal."

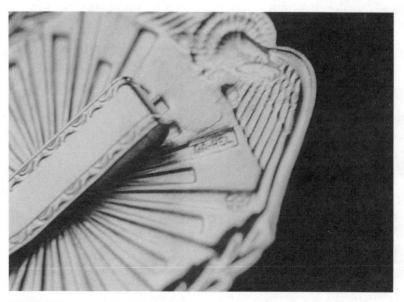

"GA-REL."

CHAPTER 4

REPRODUCTIONS

Many collector's items are reproduced, and law enforcement badges are no exception. The subject of replica badges will not be addressed negatively here, as there is a place for them. Some collectors will agree, and some will disagree.

Replicas are not bad, but have been perceived by some in a negative way because they have been sold or traded as the genuine item by someone aware that it's a replica. This includes badge collectors, antique dealers, gun dealers, military collectors and anyone else who may buy, sell and trade badges. Unfortunately, it's not always easy to recognize a replica badge—whether you're in the hobby or not. There are some things all of the above mentioned people can do to assist in identifying replicas, which we will be discussing.

First I would like to define what a replica badge is. In this hobby it's not as easy as you might think. This is a list of possible definitions, depending on your individual opinions about replicas:

This 1920s Prohibition Agent shield was made in the 1980s. The Colt, however, is authentic.
Value of badge: $15-$20

1. An unauthorized copy of a particular department's current issue badge that never passed through the department—used or not. (This may be the exact badge used by the department).

2. An authorized copy of a particular department's current issue badge that never passed through the department—used or not.

3. A copy of an obsolete style department badge.

4. A badge not officially purchased by the department or issued for duty.

5. A badge that is an "overrun" of a department order.

6. A dealer's sample badge.

7. A copy of an antique badge (may or may not be artificially aged) worn by a famous lawman, or from a famous town, i.e. Dodge City.

8. A copy of a badge from a famous law enforcement agency, i.e. Texas Rangers.

9. Movie and television "prop" badges. (This group is one of the more accepted replica areas).

10. A "parts" badge, which is assembled from existing pieces (from a manufacturer) to complete a badge.

11. A fantasy badge, which is lettered with a non-existent town or department name. (This could be considered an area all by itself.)

So how do we determine if a badge is genuine (by the definition you feel comfortable with) or a reproduction? The primary rule to follow is that there is no primary rule to follow, no one rule that will give you the answer. I wish I could tell you there was, but there just isn't. Instead, we must depend on a variety of things to help us make our determination.

Having good reference material on hand is a must. Some of the companies making high quality replica badges (which are very hard to authenticate) advertise their sales catalogs. Send for them. The more familiar you are with what reproductions are available, the easier it will be to spot them. I mentioned earlier that there is a place for replica badges. Many of the high quality replica badges I'm referring to are near exact copies of antique badges that are impossible to find, nearly impossible to find, or way too expensive if you did find one! Many of these are badges from my favorite time period—the Old West. Unable to afford the antiques, these good copies fill in parts of my collection nicely. And no, I don't represent them to onlookers as the real thing. A brief explanation on the rarity of genuine badges of our early frontier is easily understandable. This is just being realistic. After all, how many actual "Marshal" badges can exist from Tombstone, Dodge City, Abilene, Virginia City and Deadwood? Even in the heydays of these famous towns, they did not employ large numbers of lawmen. You should recognize this as a tip.

Beware of antique appearing badges with names of famous Old West locales on them. These Old West replicas were first marketed in the 1950s , probably because of the high interest in western movies at the time. Probably the two most replicated badges today are those of the Texas Rangers and United States Marshals. Finding a genuine, old or modern Texas Ranger or U.S. Marshal badge is an extremely rare occurrence. Many nice replicas of these exist, and if purchased reasonably, they make nice additions to one's collection.

Never pay big bucks for famous badges like these unless they are accompanied by good documentation/photos. Most of the high-quality replicas I've mentioned sell out of the catalog from the $38 to $65 range. No need to pay more. A second wave of high quality old west badges have made an appearance, which are just as nice as the ones previously mentioned, but you can pay a much more reasonable price for them. These can be had for $10 to $20.

Other good reference material would include photos of officer(s) wearing a badge like the one you are trying to authenticate. With a good enough photograph you should easily be able to tell if its the same style, and maybe even compare the wording. A photo may give you an approximate age of your badge, according to the·date of the photo. If the photo isn't dated, state or local historical societies can help date them. One antique badge in my collection was authenticated with the help of the department who had used it. In fact, they located a photo of the officer wearing the same badge in the 1920s , as well as the officer's name!

Law enforcement trade and association magazines can be of help also because they usually contain photos of officers. Old police association magazines help because they list names and picture officers who were working at the time. Local newspapers as well as department history books are valuable in locating photos and information. It's not uncommon for a newspaper to have written an article about the local police department receiving new badges. If you're lucky the article will be accompanied by a photo.

If your badge has a name on it, it can be checked with department rosters to find out when the officer was employed. Family members may also be of help with information and photos.

This tip is so elementary that it doesn't need listing, but I will anyway! On one occasion I received a list of badges for sale from a dealer/collector. I noticed one of the badges listed was from my home state, which interested me. It was a 5-point star with deputy sheriff and county name stamped into it with the state seal. After thinking about it, I realized that there is no county by that name here! Elementary lesson...check the alphabetical listing in an atlas to make sure there is such a place!

Another place to check for information is old city council records, which sometimes indicate the purchase of badges for a police department. These records or city inventory records may describe the badges.

Good information sources that shouldn't be overlooked are established badge collectors, who will usually help another collector if they can. If you aren't in the "collecting circle" so to speak, check an issue of *Police Collectors News*, for names to call on. The Internet is also a source for a large listing of collectors.

A highly reproduced badge is that of the U.S. Marshals.

Sometimes group photos are clear enough that close-up shots can be made. These close-ups will help identify the style of badge and possibly the inscription.   **Value: $10-$60**

"Named" badges are easier to authenticate. With the help of a sheriff's association yearbook, I found that Sheriff Roberts served Garden Co. 1944 to 1958.   **Value: $75-$100**

A fine example of a studio card photo that clearly shows the badge, "Reading 11 Police," from Pennsylvania.   **Value: $22-$30**

The author purchased this shield and tie-bar set from a family member. Sheriff Cornell served Polk Co. 1951.   **Value: $75-$100**

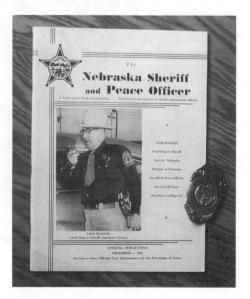

Old peace officer association magazines sometimes help in identifying badges. Some run lots of photos and some don't.   **Value: $3-$5**

A selection of contemporary big city badges, all reproductions!
Value: $10-$18

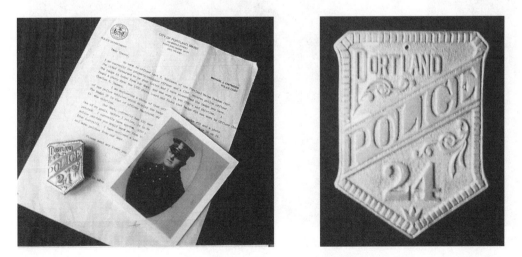

Rarely are law enforcement agencies able to help identify their old style badges. This is one of those rare occasions where "Portland Police 24" was identified as being used in the 1920s and the department provided the officer's name who used it, as well as a photo of him wearing it!
Value: $250-$300

Caution must be used in antique and collectible shops where badges are offered for sale. Oftentimes these dealers don't know if their badges are genuine or not.

Two examples of beautifully made and aged Old West replicas. One can see how these can be passed off as genuine. **Value: $10-$60**

Cheap quality reproductions such as these are plentiful. **Value: $3-$5**

No, this one wasn't dug up in Kansas. This large brass star is one of many "FOX" brand replicas that has had the ball-tips removed. These badges are available in a myriad of titles.   **Value: $3-$4**

Researching old badges is a lot of work, but can be rewarding. Going through department history books, old newspapers and photos are a good place to start.

A nicely-made replica of the rare Los Angeles Police Series 5-1/2" "diamond" badge. The replica is flat, has no hallmark, and only 220 were made.

Value: $50-$65

One of the most reproduced badges in history is the Texas Ranger badge. This one, however, is the real thing. Beware of high-quality reproductions. **Value: $1500-$2000**

CHAPTER 5

WHAT'S VALUABLE AND WHAT'S NOT

Placing values on law enforcement badges is said to be an impossibility. What's valuable to one person may not be to the next. The value a collector places on a badge is comparable to the interest that person has for the badge. Many collectors specialize in a certain catagory of badges such as: state patrol, major cities, federal, railroad, tribal or military police to name a few.

Customarily, a collector of federal badges wouldn't be interested in a state patrol badge except for the trade potential it holds. The collector may know someone who will trade him a federal for the unwanted state patrol badge he has.

The point is, the state patrol badge we're talking about still holds an inherent value, no matter if its current owner is interested in it or not. This could be said in any field of collectibles. To help give an understanding of what the hobby as a whole values, I've listed four general catagories for the sake of illustration.

The first catagory, "highly valuable" pieces should be mentioned first. They are:

This sharp 6-point star in silver with blue enamelling in the points and a color Kansas seal. **Value: $70-$85**

1. Antique badges (more than 50 yrs. old):
Antique badge named or with documentation of notable owner
Antique handmade presentation badges (more than 50 yrs.)
Antique badges with high content of gold, silver, etc., and/or adorned with precious stones
Pre-1900 handmade tin stars
U.S. Marshal & Deputy Marshal badges (documented)
Texas, Arizona & Colorado Rangers badges (documented)
Past-issue federal badges of the U.S. Secret Service, Federal Bureau of Investigation, Treasury Dept./Prohibition/Narcotics

2. Valuable badges:
Total custom die badges from large agencies, i.e. cities, counties, state agencies, railroads, tribals, federals, etc.
Semi-custom die badges from above list, those with custom seals, panels, etc. Catalog style badges from above list.
Documented badges
Catalog badges from large agencies
K-9 police dog badges

Antique military police badges (50+yrs. old)
Presidential Inaugural badges
Limited edition badges for special events,
    centennials etc.

3. General badges:
Catalog badges from police and sheriff's
    departments
Modern military police
Specials, reserves, auxilliaries, communications,
    movie props, posses

4. Low value badges:
Hat badges
Wallet/ID badges, especially if not full sized
General security badges
Toy badges
Souvenir badges
Reproductions

The above listed catagories are not meant to be all inclusive. In the same vein, the value ranges shown throughout this book do not represent every value of every badge, that would be impossible. The value ranges shown were derived from numerous advertisements and sale listings in *Police Collectors News,* lists of fellow collectors, dealers, and personal knowledge. Not everyone will agree with the values listed, and I respect their opinions. In the last several years, badge values seem to be artificially higher than is reasonable. Some collectors/dealers advertise badges from their collections at an extremely high price for the purpose of making a huge profit, or if a trade deal is presented, they'll be able to effect a better deal. Some collectors and dealers in other fields aren't knowledgeable in the values of law badges, and set inaccurate prices on them.

This work is meant to offer them a resource guide to go by to assist them in buying and selling badges. The more desirable badges are valuable for various reasons. Some of which are: the material they're made of, the department they're from, their rarity (not only because of age and scarcity), but their design (semi- or full-custom die non-catalog badge), and their documentation. Some of the most valuable badges in the hobby are those that are handmade presentation pieces with high gold content and may even

be adorned with precious gems. These would be out of the average collector's price range.

A popular but difficult area to collect is that of the Indian police. Indian police forces were established in some tribes during the 1860s and 1870s. It wasn't until 1878 that the U.S. Government instituted Indian police forces into nearly every tribe. Badges used by each tribe were as varied as any other police agency. A variety of material, shapes, and wording best describes them. The early badges are very rare and command premium prices. Contemporary Indian police badges can range from plain to fancy, which may be adorned with colorful enamelling in custom designs, and are very disirable collectibles.

The railroads provide another popular collecting field with a variety of badges marked: "Railroad Police," "Special Agent," "Special Police," and will normally be stamped with the particular railroad company name. Even though many railroads have existed, the number of railroad policemen is relatively low. Finding past issues or modern day railroad badges is a difficult task, but they are valuable pieces.

A badge that is made from a totally custom die is always a good find. Die costs increase the original cost of the badge to begin with, and custom badges are usually very attractive items. Generally it's the larger departments that can afford to issue custom die badges. Large agencies have always been popular with collectors, especially the Los Angeles, Ca. Police, who adopted a total custom die oval in 1940. This badge, called the LAPD Series 6, is one of, if not the most sought after, badge in the hobby much to the dismay of the Los Angeles Police. It is a tightly controlled badge which the LAPD has 'removed' from some hobbyists collections over the years. In addition to the sheer beauty of the shield, its popularity can in part be attributed to all of the LA police of Hollywood, most particularly the television series, "Dragnet" and "Adam-12."

Early versions of this shield were marked, "Policeman" and "Policewoman," which have been changed to the more standard title of "Police Officer." This shield is also one of the most reproduced badges in the hobby and often sells for $75 to $150 depending on the quality.

The real thing is a different story however, commanding a staggering $1000 to $1500!

State agency badges are popular with collectors, especially state highway patrol examples. State patrol badges, like most others, range from the standard catalog badge to the total custom die. Some states have a criminal investigation department that is separate from the state patrol. These are are very popular, but also very difficult to obtain. State Game Warden (also called Conservation Officers) badges are another worthwhile area to collect.

We've already established that collecting badges with old west town names on them is nearly impossible unless you consider some of the good quality reproductions now available. It is possible to find twentieth century badges from historic towns and counties. This area is also a difficult one, but the badges add great interest to one's collection.

Badges that are the least scarce and have a traditionally low value are hat badges. One of the reasons hat pieces are less desirable is rarely do they exhibit the agency name, making it difficult to nearly impossible to learn where it was used. They are commonly lettered with only, "Police," or "Patrolman," etc., and maybe a number. Hat badges with a slighty higher value would be those that feature the department name and those that are very old. The wreath badges that were so popular during the late nineteenth and early twentieth centuries do hold some value, especially if you know where it was used. This time period also saw the use of hat badges made of ribbon material. Unfortunately, the survival rate of these is very low.

Security badges have always taken a back seat to "real cop" badges and their values demonstrate this. Even though the value ranges of security badges is low, some interesting areas exist. First of all, a collector who wants to include these in his collection could start by collecting badges from the most well-known security companies. Also, many nice examples were used by guards of ammunition depots, aircraft plants and other stateside military installations during World War II.

Badges that have intentionally or accidentally been damaged usually ruin an otherwise valuable piece. I've seen officer's badges that came off in the P.D. parking lot after a few cruisers pressed them into the cement. They don't come through looking pretty! Sometimes the title or some other feature on a badge will be changed so it could be used in a different manner. A common way to change this is by grinding off the unwanted area. This is sad but it does happen, and rightfully destroys the badge's value.

Souvenir badges are available nearly everywhere along your vacation route. They are usually marked "Sheriff" or "Marshal" and feature the name of the town or attraction. Selling anywhere from $2 to $5 which is expensive considering their low quality. They are, however, only souvenir pieces and just might be a good way to get junior interested in dad's hobby. Triple A has had the "School Safety Patrol" program for many years which involves the training of students to serve at street crossings before and after school.

They are issued a safety vest and a AAA badge. These nicely made tin badges feature the ranks of "Patrolman," "Corporal," "Sergeant," "Lieutenant" and "Captain," and read "School Safety Patrol." Older versions read, "School Boy Patrol." Some law enforcement agencies had real badges made for their schools. Examples read: "School Safety Patrol," "Youth Patrol," or "School Police." These badges would make an interesting display, but are in the lower value range.

Examples of special presentation badges of 14kt and 18kt gold, some of which are adorned with jewels. **Value: $1000-$10,000**

A modern example of an Indian badge, this 7-point star is from the Yakima Tribe in Washington.
Value: $95-$120

A plain 6-point star of the Atchison, Topeka & Sante Fe Railroad. **Value: $100-$130**

These gold badges feature mounted gemstones.   **Value: $1,000-$10,000**

An older nickel-plated police badge from the Rose-bud reservation in South Dakota.
Value: $75-$100

A named nickel-plated shield from the Chicago, Burlington & Quincy Railroad.   **Value: $95-$120**

A gorgeous total custom die shield with multicolor enamel from Honolulu, Hi. Police.

Value: $400-$450

A variety of common police hat badges, none with agency name. **Value: $5-$10**

This total custom die shield features custom city seal, and red, white and blue enameling. (V.H. Blackinton Co. photo) **Value: $150-$185**

Wells Fargo, a famous company, issued these attractive badges made of a plastic material.

Value: $25-$35

Two examples of ammunition plant guard badges of WWII. The "Gopher Ordnance Works" (Minnesota) is a catalog badge with custom seal. The "U.S. Naval Ammunition Depot" (Nebraska) is a total custom die piece.

Value: $35-$45

This heavy gold-plated custom shield was used at the Martin USA bomber plant at Omaha, Nebraska during World War II. **Value: $175-$225**

This pre-1940 Omaha badge has had the lettering on the top two panels "Omaha Metropolitan," ground off, possibly for use by another agency. This greatly reduces the value of a nice antique badge.

**Value in mint condition:
$150-$175; as is: $55-$65**

The large security companies include the historic Pinkerton's, established in 1850. Past-style "Security Service" on the left, and older issue "Special Service" on the right.   **Value: $25-$30**

K-9 badges are usually mounted on some type of holder, like this leather example. The holder attaches to the dog's collar.   **Value: $65-$75**

An array of cheap souvenir badges.   **Value: $2-$4**

This Houston Police dog badge is a miniature of the regular issue. Being a major city K-9 adds to value.
Value: $70-$90

Another K-9 badge, this one from the New Hampshire State Police, gold-plated, green lettering, color seal. **Value: $95-$110**

Another local special issue badge, this one commemorating the participation of President Ronald Reagan at dedication of a new college building.

Value: $100-$125

Special issue commemorative badges are usually made in limited numbers as this Douglas, Wyoming Police circle star indicates. Sixty badges were made to commemorate the department's 100th year.

Value: $75-$90

Collecting of prison/correctional badges is another area of specialization. Not as popular as law enforcement badges, they do have a following. This example is an obsolete shield, "State Penitentiary Nebr. Lieutenant." **Value: $40-$55**

Both reproductions of the LAPD Series 6, the "Captain" (left) is a movie prop badge. The "Policeman" (right) is a foreign made replica.

Value: $85-$125

A prison hat badge with Nebraska state seal. "N.S.P.," stands for "Nebraska State Penitentiary."

Value: $18-$25

This modern shield from Beatrice, NE Police is a semi-custom piece. It is a catalog badge with a custom panel arrangement. It also notes a National Historic site which adds interest.

Value: $85-$110

This Indiana State Police shield is reverse stamped, causing the lettering to be raised. It is a total custom die shield. **Value: $250-$300**

(Indiana State Police photo)

A past issue Kansas Bureau of Investigation (KBI) eagle-top shield.　**Value: $95-$120**

This Ohio State Conservation Officer shield was used during the 1940s & 1950s.　**Value: $75-$85**

A plain eagle-top shield with plain borderless state seal, Nebraska Deputy Game Warden used in the 1930s & 1940s.　**Value: $85-$95**

A modern badge from one of the most famous towns of the Old West, Dodge City, Kansas. This gold-plated 7-point star is a nice looking catalog badge.　**Value: $95-$110**

Police agencies sometimes furnish real badges for school safety patrols. Shown are Memphis, Tn., Duluth, Mn., and San Diego, Ca.   **Value: $8-$12**

Teardrop shield with blue reverse enamel panels and color state seal. A very nice state badge.
Value: $95-$120

This is a modern Union Pacific shield, two-tone plated nickel and gold.   **Value: $110-$125**

This plain eagle-top shield lettered "Special Officer" would hold limited interest for collectors.
Value: $10-$14

Resembling a hat badge, this Wackenhut security is a custom die breast badge. **Value: $25-$30**

An advertising badge from a tobacco company issued in the early 1990s. **Value: $3-$5**

Classic examples of Hollywood prop badges. These teardrop styles marked "Metropolitan Police" have been used on countless TV and motion picture productions. These badges are fairly difficult to obtain, as the prop rental companies prefer to keep them for renting out instead of selling them. **Value: $65-$85**

Police K-9 "Sarge" and the badge that he wears.
Value: $75-$90

This fine police pistol match medal was awarded in 1936. Shooting medals that identify the department, year and type of match are scarce.
Value: $110-$115

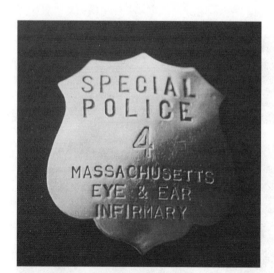

Plain nickel-plated shield from a state eye & ear infirmary. Unusual. **Value: $25-$35**

A unique circle 5-point star with ball tips on the outside of the circle. These have been used in the Washington & Oregon areas. Good badge, but "Reserve" designation reduces value.

Value: $60-$70

Nickel sunburst with plain Louisiana seal, "Port Commission 49 Harbor Patrol." This badge is interesting being a 'harbor patrol' and it's from New Orleans, a major city. **Value: $100-$125**

Generally, law badge collectors don't collect fire badges unless they have an enforcement title such as this "Fire Police" eagle-top sunburst.

Value: $25-$35

Toy badges officially authorized by television programs. The "Matt Dillon" is from the TV show "Gunsmoke," and is hallmarked, "c. 1959 CBS Inc." The "Wyatt Earp" badge is from the TV show, "The Life & Legend of Wyatt Earp," and is hallmarked, "c. 1957 Wyatt Earp Enter." **Value: $65-$70**

This plain shield with cut-out 5-point star features a tongue-style catch and a "C.D. REESE" hallmark. The badge dates to the late 1930s. Someone has handstamped a number on the star. The badge is old and hallmarked, with "Special" designation.   **Value: $20-$25**

This pre-1950 company guard badge has partial coverage of rust. It is hallmarked "Irvine-Jachens S.F.," wire pin back.   **Value: $15-$20**

Although not a law enforcement badge, this custom shield may be of interest to special groups who collect plant agricultural officer's items.   **Value: $50-$55**

Fire damages badge value as shown by this North Platte, NE, eagle-top sunburst.   **Value: $10-$15**

One of the more unusual badge shapes is this round "Deputy Sheriff 258 Fayette Co. Pa." Old wire pin back and no hallmark. **Value: $35-$45**

A gold-plated eagle-top shield marked on top ribbon, "C.B.& Q.," and "Special Agent Burlington R.R." Post merger badge of the two railroads.
Value: $85-$150

An annual special event badge from the, "Queen of the Cowtowns," Dodge City, Kansas. These badges were available for each year of their "Longhorn Drive." Custom die 5-point balled-tip star with green enameling. **Value: $30-$40**

A custom die shield with state shape (NE) on top. "State Sheriff" designates statewide authority as opposed to county authority of deputy county sheriff. **Value: $100-$125**

Game warden or "conservation officer" badges are a specialty area of collecting. The 6-point star is from Illinois, the eagle top shield is currently used in Nebraska.　　**Value: $45-$55**

"Merchant police" were civilians paid by businessmen to patrol their properties. A somewhat unusual collecting field.　　**Value: $25-$30**

Two obsolete badges which were used in the Village of Juniata, Nebraska. The plain 6-point star saw service in the 1950s, while the 7-point star is from the 1960s.

Value: $25-$35

This large (3-1/2") 6-point star would be hard to miss. **Value: $20-$30**

Agents of the Nebraska Liquor Commission were issued these shields before being absorbed by the Nebraska State Patrol. By law, the 'Deputy State Sheriff' appointment is what gave the agents statewide jurisdiction. **Value: $40-$65**

An eagle-top sunburst shield with applied numbers from Kentucky, and a custom die shield from a now defunct Boston agency, the "Metropolitan Police."

Value: $25-$35

A metropolitan-style shield with an applied, enameled coat-of-arms.   **Value: $35-$50**

An impressive 7-point star with a custom center seal and applied reverse enamel rank panel. Many modern badges display their locale's history in the design of their badges and seals. **Value: $85-$95**

Nickel-plated oval shield with applied 7-point star. Another agency which has statewide police powers.

Value: $80-$125

A 'named' sunburst shield with plain brass Colorado state seal. A good state investigative agency piece.   **Value: $80-$120**

Plain 6-point star from Chicago, Burlington & Quincy Railroad.   **Value: $115-$150**

C. B. & Q. railroad "Special Police" 5-point balled tip star with applied round panel.

Value: $90-$140

This 6-point balled tip star has a large round applied panel and plain NE seal. **Value: $75-$90**

Badges of the American Automobile Association (AAA) for use by school safety patrols. Ranks shown are: patrolman, corporal, sergeant, lieutenant and captain. The bottom right hand badge is an older vintage showing school "boy" patrol.

Value: $4-$8

A custom die badge from a major city, this Detroit badge is issued to "Reserves." Regular officer badges are usually more valuable.

Value: $45-$65

This eagle-top shield is from a western state, New Mexico, which are collectable. **Value: $75-$90**

Badges from famous places always add value, like this modern badge from the "town too tough to die," Tombstone, AZ. **Value: $95-$140**

"Watchman" title is a variation, this one C. B. & Q. railroad. **Value: $85-$95**

Badges from the well-known Burns Int'l Detective and Security Services.   **Value: $25-$35**

A similar gold-plated custom shield used by a contracted security company during the 1940s-50s.
Value: $75-$85

A circle 5-point star (1950s-60s) of the Union Pacific Railroad.   **Value: $125-$150**

CHAPTER 6

CITY POLICE & COUNTY SHERIFF BADGES

Sir Robert Peel was responsible for instituting the first organized police force, the Metropolitan Police of London in 1829. Before that time, England had many problems depending on the Army to quell riots and handle ordinary criminals. In 1822, when Robert Peel was appointed to office of home secretary, he became responsible for internal security. With this appointment, he was ordered to establish a police force that would relieve the army of handling riots and criminals. For the next seven years, Peel fought major obstacles. The average citizen, as well as Parliament, feared the police would take away freedom from the people. At that time, English criminal law was cruelly strict and desperately needed reform. Peel intended his reform plan for the entire country, but these obstacles convinced him to focus on the city of London first. After that was completed, he planned to extend his reform to the rest of the country, which eventually was accomplished. The English Parliament passed the Metropolitan

Obsolete style Beatrice Nebraska Chief's shield. It is gold-plated with color state seal. **Value: $40-$55**

Police Act of 1829 which opened the door for the recruitment of an adequate number of constables, who would enforce the new criminal code.

Less than ten years later, the Boston Police Department was formed in 1838. Boston is recognized as the oldest police force in the United States. Most early U.S. city police forces were modeled after the British example.

The badges most often encountered are those used by regular city police and county sheriff's departments. The variety is almost unlimited because it was and still is somewhat common for a newly-appointed police chief, or newly elected sheriff to issue new style badges. This is done for various reasons which include maintaining individuality and to keep his predecessor from continuing to use his old badge.

Titles one will find when looking for police badges are numerous. Rank structures were developed similar to the military. The starting rank of a police department would usually be "Patrolman," then "Corporal," "Sergeant," "Lieutenant," "Captain," "Deputy or Assistant Chief," and "Chief." Larger agencies sometimes use additional ranks while smaller ones don't use all of those listed. Because of the increasing number of females in police work, badges that read "Policewoman" were issued in some agencies, but gradually a uniform title came into use such as, "Officer" or "Police Officer."

In the nineteenth century, large city agencies were most often called police departments. However, the tiny villages that popped up eventually hired a town constable or city marshal. During the late 1800s, some towns replaced the title of City Marshal with "Chief of Police." As stated earlier, the first badges simply read "Marshal," "Deputy Marshal," "Police," etc. Special position designations were not common but one that was in use, "Patrol Driver," denoted an officer who operated the horse drawn paddy wagons and later the motorized versions.

The collector will find numerous badges imprinted with "Special Officer" or "Special Police." "Specials" were often utilized by towns that didn't need a full-time staff of more than one or two. One very notable "Special" was Wyatt Earp's brother Morgan.

According to Tombstone City Marshal Virgil Earp, who testified at the O.K. Corral inquest, Morgan Earp wore a badge inscribed with "Special Police" during the gunfight with the cowboys. The special is a part-time (paid or not) person that may or may not have prior law enforcement training, who is hired for a specific time or event. In the old days this position could hold full arrest powers, depending on the wishes of the marshal or chief. Police chiefs sometimes gave this type of badge to their close friends to give them special privileges of sorts. Some "Special Police" badges came from the maker with a date stamped on the front that indicated the time that the position expired. Other titles commonly seen are "Auxiliary" and "Reserve" police. Auxiliary police sometimes assisted police departments with extra work during wartime and civil defense duties. The police auxiliary usually had more of an official connection to the department.

In modern times, "reserve" police officers are those who are part of an official segment of the department. Reserve officers receive mandated state training before they can go to work. On duty, they have full powers like the regular officer. The reserves could be called "volunteers" because they earn a token $1.00 per year in most places!

Generally speaking the hobby doesn't value "Special," "Auxiliary" or "Reserve" marked badges as high as regular officer's badges.

In early England, the countryside was policed by sheriffs who represented the king and local constables. The old office of sheriff came to America from England when counties were first established in Virginia in 1634. During the early nineteenth century, these positions crossed the Mississippi river as frontiersmen and settlers moved west expanding the United States. Before counties were established in the west, "territorial sheriffs" were appointed. A territorial sheriff would commonly be responsible for a large area, which would later break up into 8 to 10 counties or more! A badge with this inscription would be a very rare and valuable piece.

It wasn't uncommon through the years for law enforcement officers to supply their own badges, which resulted in a variety of styles being used. Officers of the same department sometimes wore different style badges. In recent years, some states have enacted laws that require all of the sheriff's departments in the state to wear the same specified badge style. One example is Nebraska, where legislation was passed stating, "County Sheriffs and their deputies, when on duty, shall be dressed in a distinctive uniform, and seven-point star badge bearing state seal, rank and county, gold in color for sheriff and deputies of the rank of sergeant or above, silver in color for deputies under the rank of sergeant."

Common designations on sheriff's department's badges are "Deputy Sheriff," "Chief Deputy Sheriff," "Undersheriff," the latter two being equivalent to a Deputy Chief of Police. Being an elected official, sheriff's gave out "Honorary" or "Special" deputy sheriff badges to their supporters as a political favor.

"Specials" did assist when needed for duties the regular officers wouldn't have time for. This could be anything from guarding voting precincts to providing added firepower against a gangster's crime spree.

Besides the regular department issued badges, there exists a large number of "personal" badges that the officer purchases him/herself for use in a wallet, ID case or on a belt clip. Sometimes officers buy a badge identical to their "issue" piece, or sometimes a smaller-sized badge that fits better in a wallet. These badges may have the officer's name on them, which generally detracts from the value on modern badges, unless of course, the officer is famous for one reason or another.

As far as collecting sheriff's badges geographically, you'll find them in every state except Alaska because as there are no counties in that state. The Alaska State Troopers along with town and city police provide law enforcement for the

49th state. The State of Louisiana has "parishes" instead of counties. Parishes were established as administrative units of the Roman Catholic Church during Spanish rule of the area. A badge may read, "Deputy Sheriff-Terrebonne Parish."

Some believe that historically, the star badge represents sheriffs and the shield badge represents the police. This is the case in certain areas of the country today, but I've been unable to substantiate this as any kind of absolute trend through time. During my research and years of collecting, I've seen many sheriff's shields and many police stars. During the 1930s, 1940s, and 1950s in Nebraska, sheriffs usually wore shields. Many police departments in California and Illinois, for example, have used stars for many years.

Most of the original gold plating has vanished from years of hard use on this old shield. It is a good example of legitimate use and age. Some detail on the state seal has worn off.   **Value: $65-$80**

This ornate little shield is from the ski resort, Estes Park, Colorado. It is nickel-plated and features a large embossed star for a center seal.
                    Value: $85-$90

An example of a 7-point star with balled tips. Seal is the "Great Seal of Nebraska." Lettering is hard-enamel block-style. Modern badge made by Entenmann-Rovin. **Value: $65-$70**

Medium size 6-point star, "Deputy Sheriff Orange Co." An old stock badge. **Value: $55-$65**

"Undersheriff Smith County," a nice gold 6-point star from Kansas, with blue enameling in points and blue hard-enamel Roman-style lettering. Finish is dull from use. **Value: $85-$90**

Older badges that have been used should show plating worn off evenly across the badge face. Applied numbers in the center usually show the worst wear as they stick out the furthest from the badge front. This Beatrice, NE badge, used in the 1950s-60s, shows this wear. **Value $65-80**

An unusual shape for a law badge, this special deputy sheriff is known as a "maltese cross" shape, most commonly used by fire departments. **Value: $45-$55**

A current Nebraska deputy sheriff star, a 7-point with "Great Seal" of Nebraska, sheriff's numbers start with nine, then its county number, then deputies number. **Value: $75-$85**

Eagle-top shield that features a large plain, borderless state seal. No doubt a patrolman's shield changed for use by the chief. **Value: $60-$75**

Badges come in all sizes, as this photo shows. Both have pin-backs.
Value: (left) $40-$65   Value: (right) $20-$35

This shield appears to be a custom die piece, but it actually is a catalog badge. It has blue and white enameling covering half of the front.

Value: $70-$90

A semi-custom teardrop shield featuring a custom panel arrangement. This piece is two-tone, with gold back and silver panels. A nice chief's badge.

Value: $85-$100

Brown reverse enamel panels enhance this gold 7-point star along with a large custom county center seal, also in color enameling. A nice modern Arizona star.   **Value: $80-$115**

A plain 7-point star currently in use. It has an antique bronze finish.   **Value: $30-$40**

Good representative deputy sheriff star from California, with bear in center, this one from San Bernardino County. Hallmarked "Larsco Products Los Angeles, Cal."   **Value: $125-$175**

An example of a 5-point star commonly used statewide in Florida sheriff's departments. They have full-color borderless Fla. center seals.

Value: $30-$45

Even though this star is a 'Special Deputy,' it is an old and unique style. Used in the 1930s & 40s. Wire pin back.

Value: $130-$165

"Deputy Sheriff Custer County," 5-point balled-tip star from South Dakota. Black hard enamel is used on letters as well as the points of the star.

Value: $65-$80

Another catalog badge, this eagle-top shield has applied numbers instead of a state seal. State is, however, identified.

Value: $35-$40

A finely-detailed "Great Seal" adorns this medium-sized eagle-top shield.　　**Value: $25-$35**

Eagle-top catalog shield with plain Mississippi seal. Interesting rank denoted on badge, "Detective Sergt."　　**Value: $60-$80**

"Chief Police Hot Springs S.D." Nice eagle-top shield from South Dakota.　　**Value: $70-$85**

Large shield with inscription, "Police Washington County Colorado."　　**Value: $35-$45**

This sheriff's shield from Lincoln County, NE features a blue enamel rim seal and dull gold finish.
Value: $65-$70

Black enamel rim state seal was used on this nickel-plated eagle-top shield. "Special Deputy Sheriff Franklin Co. Nebr."
Value: $20-$25

Sheriff Lyle B. Olson served from 1951 to 1966. Evidently he used this shield for most of that time, judging by the wear.
Value: $65-$75

This old eagle-top shield was originally two-tone gold and silver. It shows much wear and reads "Captain Grand Island Police Nebr."
Value: $55-$65

A plain 6-point star with fancy lettering not often found on badges. This adds interest even though it is a "special." **Value: $50-$65**

Plain shield, "Deputy Sheriff Randolph County Ind."
Value: $35-$45

Gold-plated eagle-top sunburst with plain border-less Colorado seal. "Chief Police Loveland, Colo." Chief Charles K. Steele used this piece, date unknown. **Value: $65-$70**

Common catalog eagle-top shield, another "Chief," used by W. E. Christensen in Minden, NE.
Value: $45-$55

Very little finish is left on this small eagle-top shield. It was used in the 1950s by a clerk-matron.
Value: $18-$25

Gold-plated eagle-top shield, "C.L. Morrison Sheriff Chase County Nebr."
Value: $30-$40

Circle 5-point star, "Special Deputy Sheriff Scotts Bluff County." Plain NE seal applied to star.
Value: $22-$25

"Clyde F. Garrett Sheriff Hayes County Nebr." Used from 1962-1977 Gold-plated with plain NE seal.
Value: $45-$60

Medium-sized eagle-top shield, "Sioux City Iowa Police 54." **Value: $35-$40**

A named nickel-plated eagle-top shield, with plain brass Colorado seal. "Under Sheriff" rank interesting. **Value: $45-$65**

This shield with applied center "Chief" disc, was used in Holdrege, NE. **Value: $35-$45**

Another turn-of-the-century style, this example from Florida, circa 1950s. **Value: $30-$35**

Modern teardrop shield with blue hard enamel lettering and full-color state seal. "Chief Kensington Police," (Kansas).   **Value: $75-$85**

Obsolete 7-point star of the Las Vegas, Nevada Police. The city and county have combined and the department is now called "Metropolitan Police." **Value: $200-$300**

The finish is so bad on this shield, it's hard to read, "Sheriff Morgan County" (CO).   **Value: $50-$60**

"Chicago Police Sergt. (Retired) 478" This 6-point star features the Chicago city seal in center.
Value: $80-$95

Older eagle-top shield, "Deputy Sheriff Sarpy County, Neb." Lettering is a combination of Roman and block styles.
Value: $55-$65

Large "pie plate" 6-point star, "Cicero Police" on raised letter panel, and "1489" in applied copper numbers.
Value: $85-$125

A nickel-plated shield with applied 5-point star in center. This Augusta Police Detective badge is from Georgia.
Value: $75-$110

This eagle-top sunburst shield was used in Fort Lupton, Colorado. It is nickel-plated and features plain Colorado seal. **Value: $35-$45**

This nickel-plated eagle-top shield from Tampa, Florida Police features large applied numbers. **Value: $55-$65**

Stars are popular with Chicago area police departments. This example is a nickel-plated 5-point star with plain Illinois seal. **Value: $65-$75**

Buffalo, New York wear these custom die eagle-top shields. They feature raised lettering and an image of a running buffalo. The very top panel is not raised, to allow each badge to be stamped with a different number. **Value: $85-$125**

A nickel-plated 5-point balled-tip star, with "Great Seal." **Value: $45-$55**

Plain 6-point balled-tip star with applied state seal. This piece was used in the1940s & 1950s. **Value: $45-$65**

Current issue shield of the Lincoln, NE Police Dept. Nickel-plated with color "State of" seal. A nice state capitol police shield. **Value: $85-$120**

"Sheriff Jefferson County," plain 6-point star used by Sheriff Frank Knocke in the 1950s. **Value: $75-$100**

This 5-point balled-tip star is gold-plated with plain state seal, soft-enamel block letters.

Value: $22-$35

This modern 7-point star was used in the 1950s & 60s. Many small towns have lost their city marshals because of funding and contract with county sheriffs.

Value: $30-$45

The center seal came off this eagle-top sunburst from Brighton, Colorado. Good rank, "Ass't. Chief," but loss of seal harms value.

Value: $35-$45

Old-style eagle-top shield from Cheyenne, Wyoming with applied numbers.

Value: $100-$125

Fancy shield with pierced star, "Creston 3 Police" was used in Iowa.   **Value: $45-$55**

A named eagle-top shield, circa 1960s.
Value: $25-$30

Shield with plain Kansas seal, "Deputy Sheriff Rooks County Kansas."   **Value: $35-$50**

Eagle-top shield with plain seal and owners initials on bottom panel.   **Value: $18-$24**

Gold-plated eagle-top shield, "Deputy Sheriff Dodge County Nebr." **Value: $35-$40**

Much wear is evident on this small eagle-top shield from Kimball County. Top panel was left blank. **Value: $22-$25**

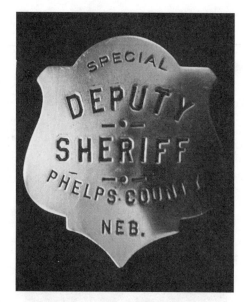

Plain shield, "Special Deputy Sheriff Phelps County Neb." **Value: $22-$30**

Sheriff Wendall Hills used this eagle-top shield from 1947-1963, in Sheridan County, Nebr. **Value: $65-$85**

"Deputy Sheriff 2 Lancaster Co." Plain shield used in the county of the
state capitol. (Ne.) **Value: $35 -$45**

Dull gold finish, hard blue-enamel block lettering
and a plain borderless state seal makes this a nice
older shield. "Sheriff Keya Paha County."
Value: $65-$85

George Welker was Sheriff of Cherry County,
Nebraska from 1959-1967. His nice eagle-top shield
has a combination of Roman and block style lettering. **Value: $65-$75**

A popular eagle-top shield since before the turn-of-the-century. "Sheriff Garden County Neb."
Value: $55-$65

Plain 6-point star used by Reserve Police officers in San Francisco, Ca. Regular officers use a similar 7-point star.
Value: $55-$65

This Denver, Colorado Special Police shield was used in the 1920s and is hallmarked, "Sachs-Lawlor Denver."
Value: $95-$125

Plain 7-point star, "San Jose R549 Police." "R" designation means reserve.
Value: $40-$50

"Marshall Kensington Kansas," 7-point balled-tip star. Spelling of the title "Marshall" with the double "L" is unusual.   **Value: $45-$55**

Total custom die major city shield, with reverse enamel top panels, "Boston Police Detective."
Value: $120-$140

"Traffic Div. 29 Lincoln Police Nebr." State capitol city shield from the 1950s.   **Value: $70-$90**

Obsolete issue Kansas City, Mo. Police patrolman's shield. It is a custom die and is virtually the same as current issue except title changed to "Officer" and color seal added.   **Value: $65-$80**

Gold-plated eagle-top shield, "Assistant Police Chief Madison Nebr.," with full-color state seal.
Value: $40-$55

'Named' nickel eagle-top shield with applied brass star in center. "Deputy Sheriff Tooele County Utah."
Value: $75-$90

Red Willow Co. Nebraska Sheriff's badge bearing the name "Jim Short," who was sheriff from 1953 to 1987.
Value: $65-$75

Nickel-plated eagle-top shield with raised letter panel and applied copper numbers. "Chicago Special Police Patrolman 5972."
Value: $45-$55

This gold-plated 5-point star features an applied disc panel and horse and rider figure. "Posse" badges are a variation in collecting sheriff's badges. **Value: $40-$55**

Eagle-top shield from Missouri features a plain state seal. This "Deputy Marshal" shield was used in the 1950s. **Value: $45-$65**

This eagle-top sunburst shield is named and was used historic Cheyenne, Wyoming. **Value: $85-$100**

The following is an assortment of post cards with a police motif. They date from the early 1900s.
Value: $.75-$5 ea.

Known as a "pie plate," this 6-point Chicago star is made of thick German silver and is heavy! It features a panel with raised letters, city seal and applied copper numbers. This style was used in the Windy City from 1905 to 1955. As it was used over a long time period, examples will be found that are very old and some that aren't. New remakes of this badge are available. These facts explain wide value range. **Value: $55-$200**

This fifty-four-year-old shield shows use and a natural patina. It was used by Sheriff A.L. Porter in "Hitchcock" County, NE, from 1943 to 1954. **Value: $85-$90**

Total custom die shield with reverse enamel panels and custom city seal. "Police North Attleboro Patrolman 39." **Value: $90-$120** (Blackinton photo)

This handsome teardrop shield is nickel-plated and features hard enamel Roman-style letters. **Value: $55-$65**

Twentieth century generic deputy sheriff star, possibly used until new deputies could buy their own badge. **Value: $25-$30**

Modern named star, gold-plated with full-color state seal. **Value: $25-$30**

Large size badge used on a "Bobbie Helmet", called a "helmet plate." This one is from the West Yorkshire Constabulary.
Value: $10-$18

A catalog shield featuring a 5-point star disc center seal. "Police Ft. Morgan, Colo."
Value: $55-$65

AMT Tijuana Border Police 1949 Ford. (1/25
Value: $35-$45

mples of the popular 1/43 scale Road Champs cars, (left to right) New Orleans Police, Royal Canadian

The gold plating on this shield is very dull with age. It appears that there were applied letters on the bottom panel at one time. This style is more commonly used as a hat badge. **Value: $35-$45**

A variation in deputy sheriff badges, this one has a "rescue squad" designation. **Value: $35-$45**

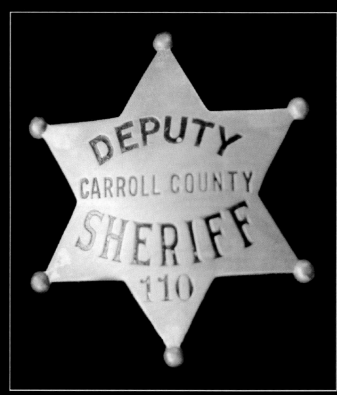

Nice example of an older 6-point star from Iowa. Most of the nickel finish has worn off. **Value: $90-$110**

A finely done 1941 Chevrolet Michigan State Police in 1/43 by Durham Automotive Miniatures. Markings are correct for the era represented. **Value: $75-$100**

The state seal on this medium-sized 5-point star has been badly worn. **Value: $30-$40**

Quite possibly the most popular unit patch to collect is the police K-9. These units have made a major comeback after the difficult 1960s, with even small departments organizing a dog unit. Large selection of patches available. **Value: $3-$6**

Police Patrol Station Department of Electricity Chicago. Cathedral pedestal (83" high) mounted call box. Cast iron & steel, circa 1900. **Value: $975-$1500** (Photo courtesy of Don Vessey.)

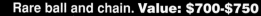

Rare ball and chain. Value: $700-$750

Michigan State Police plate. **Value: $25-$30**

Custom die eagle-top sunburst shield is dull nickel with red, hard enamel lettering. This obsolete style badge is large, measuring 3-1/4" high and 2-3/4" wide. It was used from 1966-1968. Value: $95-$110

Metropolitan Police, London, England "bobby helmet."
Value: $75-$85 old style

The current issue U.S. Marshal badge was issued in 1980. It is a custom die, circle 5-point star. This style more closely reflects the historical significance of the U.S. Marshals. (U.S. Marshal's Service photo)

A 1985 Presidential Inaugural used by the Smithsonian Institution Special Police. **Value: $85-$100**

The Game of Dragnet board game, 1950s. From the popular TV program. **Value: $25-$40**

Police statues can be found in about every size, configuration and material imaginable. Shown are examples made of plastic, porcelain, and pewter. **Value: $3.50-$30**

1937 Chevrolet sedan Delivery, Cleveland Police Dept. (Liberty Set #2) **Value: $25-$30**

1940 Ford
with
c "Sheriff"
gs, also in
cale.
: $10-$12

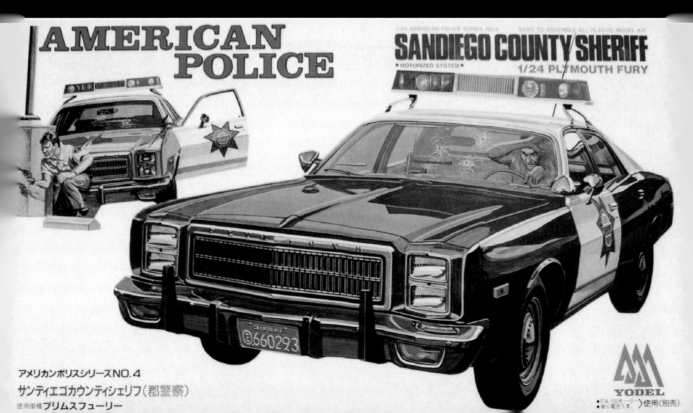

This example is one of Ertl's 1/43
scale vehicles, a 1930 Chevy pan
Chicago Police. **Value: $15-$18**

AMERICAN POLICE

SANDIEGO COUNTY SHERIFF
1/24 AMERICAN POLICE SERIES NO.4   EASY TO ASSEMBLE ALL PLASTIC MODEL KIT
• MOTORIZED SYSTEM •   1/24 PLYMOUTH FURY

CALIFORNIA 660293

アメリカンポリスシリーズNO.4
サンディエゴカウンティシェリフ（郡警察）
使用車種 プリムスフューリー

YODEL
•FA-134モーター〉使用電池1本
•単1電池1本〉使用（別売）

Revell Harley-Davidson 1200 Electra Glide California Highway Patrol bike. (1/8)
Value: $35-$40

Revell C.H.i.Ps Z-28 CHP Chase Car. (1/25)
Value: $15-$18

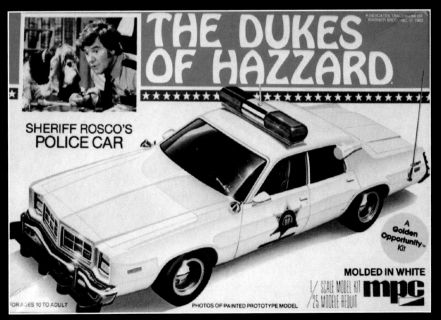

MPC The Dukes of Hazzard Roscoe's Police Car. (1/25)
Value: $25-$30

This nice old circle five point star features the halmark; "C.D. REESE 57 WARREN, NY" on back which indicates it was used in the 1930s.
Value: $85-$100

Gold-plated teardrop eagle-top shield, "Pacific Fleet Amphibious Force US Police Petty Officer Chief." A fine example of a WWII navy badge. **Value: $165-$215**

U.S. Coast Guard Tactical Law Enforcement Team patch. **Value: $4-$5**

Coast Guard Special Agent badge patch. **Value: $8-$10**

The current issue
Pinkerton Security
Service Shield.
Value: $25-$30

West Virginia State Police, "Cadet" patch.
Value: $4-$5

West Virginia State Police, "EMS Pilot" patch.
Value: $6-$8

Prior to 1937, the governor of Nebraska was directly responsible for statewide law enforcement. He carried a badge that read, "Chief-Law Enforcement Division." The officers who actually worked in the field carried these 6-point stars marked, "State Agent." **Value: $120-$150**

Air Support Unit patch of the National Police of Ireland, the Garda Siochana. **Value: $12-$14**

Unusually-shaped catalog badge. "Special Deputy

An example of Roman-style lettering. **Value: $85-$95**

CHAPTER 7

STATE POLICE &
HIGHWAY PATROL BADGES

State police and highway patrol (SP/HP) agencies got their start in the early 20th century. Organized for varying reasons, the invention of the automobile had a lot to do with it. The rapidly increasing mobility of the masses, criminal included, demonstrated a dire need for such agencies. Some had only traffic enforcement powers, leaving criminal work for others. Some SP/HP agencies started with full police powers, as are most of them today.

The past and current style badges of these agencies are very popular. We should keep in mind, however, that most states control their current issue badges by state law, which prevents reproducing and possession of the badges by civilians. Strict department regulations also help control the state's property. A wise collector will search out the many obsolete styles that have been used by SP/HP agencies over the years. Like any area of badges, SP/HP agencies have used both catalog badges as well as custom die badges.

Gold-plated eagle-top shield, "50th Anniversary Kansas Highway Patrol 1937-1987" commemorative badge issued for wear in 1987.
Value: $100-$125

There is a variety of the two types still in use today.

A collector will see a variety of wording on these badges, depending on the name of the agency. Some are, "State Police," "State Highway Police," "Courtesy Patrol," "State Patrol," "Highway Patrol," "Highway Safety Patrol," "State Highway Patrol," "State Traffic Patrol," "State Traffic Police," "State Motor Patrol," "Highway Department Patrol" and "Safety Patrol." Several of these agencies went through one or more changes in the department name which explains the variety listed. Some of these are current and some are obsolete.

Titles when included will usually be, "Patrol-man," "Traffic Officer," "Officer" and "Trooper." Military type ranks will appear on SP/HP badges also. It should be noted that surprisingly not all SP/HP agencies use breast badges! The states of New York, New Jersey, Rhode Island, Pennsylvania, and Missouri use only hat and ID badges. If your goal is to collect a badge from each SP/HP, you can come very close using obsolete hat and

ID badges.

Once complete, your collection will number 49, not 50. The reason is that the state of Hawaii has no state police agency. Instead, they have county police forces, a state sheriff, and the Honolulu Police Department. Because of the popularity of this area, collectors should be aware of the many SP/HP reproductions on the market. The difficulty and expense in obtaining SP/HP badges once again justifies the use of good quality reproductions to fill spots in a collection, at least until an original is located.

Nickel-plated, eagle-top shield, "Nebraska Safety Patrol Sergeant." Used from agency's inception in 1937 to 1967, when name was changed to "State Patrol." **Value: $125-$150**

Nickel-plated eagle-top shield, "Patrolman Auxiliary Police Ohio State Patrol 4668" Auxiliary was organized in 1942 to help fill reduced manpower in the highway patrol because of WWII. This group continues today, but on a much smaller scale.

Value: $75-$85

"Lt. Colonel Nebraska State Patrol 46." Current issue style, gold-plated, reverse enamel panels and color state seal. Badge used by C. P. Karthauser, who later became colonel (Superintendent) of the N.S.P. **Value: $150-$200**

Custom state-shaped shield, "Sergeant 63 Louisiana State Police," features red enamel seal and letters. Used from the 1940s-1960s. **Value: $100-$150**

Hat badge used by Nebraska Safety Patrol, 1937-1967. **Value: $25-$35**

"Highway Safety Patrol Mississippi Dispatcher 227". Ms. Highway Patrol badges are difficult to find. This one would be worth more with "Trooper" Designation. **Value: $165-$175**

Gold-plated eagle top shield, "Sergeant Iowa Highway
Patrol" in 1973.   **Value: $125-$135**

Nickel-plated sunburst shield with color state seal,
"Trooper Arkansas State Police 44," older issue.
                    Value: $100-$150

Total custom die hat shield with raised letters,
"Missouri State Highway Patrol." Used from the
1930s-1950s.   **Value: $85-$120**

Gold-plated winged-wheel shield, "California Highway Patrol". Current C.H.P. hat badge shown on obsolete style cap.   **Value: $75-$85**

Custom die 5-point star with black reverse enamel 'steering wheel," and black hard-enamel letters. "Driver Examiner 77 Washington State Patrol."
Value: $50-$70

Hat badge made of aluminum, circa 1925 "State Highway Patrol," State of Washington.
Value: $85-$115

"Trooper Department Public Safety Highway Patrol," gold-plated 7-point star with color seal. Past issue star of the South Dakota Highway Patrol.
Value: $185-$210

CHAPTER 8

FEDERAL AGENCY BADGES

Badges of the United States government are some of the most valuable and sought after badges in the hobby. They can also be the most hazardous to collect. The reason being United States Code, Title 18, Section 700 which relates to insignia. Section 701, official badges, identification cards, other insignia, "Whoever manufactures, sells, or possesses any badge, identification card, or other insignia, of the design prescribed by the head of any department or agency of the United States for use by any officer or employee thereof, or any colorable imitation thereof, or photographs, prints, or in any other manner makes or executes any engraving, photograph, print or impression in the likeness of any such badge, identification card, or other insignia, or any colorable imitation thereof, except as authorized under regulations made pursuant to law, shall be fined not more than $250 or imprisoned not more than six months, or both. Sounds like a pretty good reason to me to avoid "current issue" federal badges. That's okay, because many obsolete styles do exist which are fine pieces. I've

The Security Division of the Joint Chiefs of Staff issued this Presidential Inaugural in 1989. **Value: $90-$110**

given a few examples of past agency names and titles used to illustrate how some of the old style badges would read.

To illustrate the expanse of this area of badge collecting, the following is a partial listing of U.S. Government police agencies:

• Bureau of Alcohol, Tobacco and Firearms (Originally Internal Revenue Service, who formed "Alcohol, Tobacco Tax Unit," then "Bureau of Alcohol, Tobacco and Firearms.")

• U.S. Army Criminal Investigation Command
• Internal Revenue Service
• Defense Investigative Service
• National Park Service-Rangers
• Bureau of Indian Affairs (Originally the "Indian Police Service")
• Drug Enforcement Administration (Originally "Bureau of Revenue" in 1914 had responsibility. In about 1930, the "Bureau of Narcotics" was formed and then changed to "Bureau of Narcotics and Dangerous Drugs." In 1973, it finally became the "Drug Enforcement Admin.")

- Federal Aviation Administration
- Federal Bureau of Investigation (Originally
   "Bureau of Investigation" 1908-1933, then
   "Division of Investigation" 1933-1934, then
   "Federal Bureau of Investigation"
   1935-present.)
- Federal Protective Service
- Fish & Wildlife Service
- Forest Service
- Department of Defense
- U.S. Navy Naval Investigative Service
- Office of Inspector General
- U.S. Air Force Office of Special Investigations
- Postal Inspection Service
- Dept. of the Treasury
   (Old style badges may include these titles:
   "Bureau of Prohibition Agent"; "U.S. Prohi-
   bition Service Treasury Department"; "Agent
   Treasury Department."
- U.S. Bureau of Narcotics
   ("Narcotic Agent U.S. Treasury Dept.")
- Dept. of the Treasury Police- U.S. Secret Service
- U.S. Secret Service Uniformed Division
   (Originally "White House Police," then
   "Executive Protective Service,"
   now U.S.S.S. Uniformed Division.)
- U.S. Capitol Police
- U.S. Customs Service
- U.S. Marshal's Service
- U.S. Park Police (Originally "Park Watch")
- U.S. Secret Service
- U.S. Supreme Court Police

Another type of federal badge that is highly collectible is the specially issued presidential inaugural badge. The first inaugural badges were issued in 1937 by the Metropolitan Washington D.C. police, to other major city police officers who came to Washington to assist with crowd control during the inaugural activities. Since that time, these special badges have been issued by the D.C. P.D. every year except 1945. Through the following years, this idea became very popular. Nearly every federal police agency in the D.C. area now issues special badges to their officers at inaugural time. Currently, over 50 federal, state, and local agencies issue inaugural badges.

Named, nickel-plated eagle-top shield, "Matthew J. Gress Narcotic U.S. Agent." The Bureau of Narcotics was formed in 1930 and re-organized in the 1960s.   **Value: $250-$275**

Custom die eagle-top shield, "United States Capitol Police 510" 1977 issue.   **Value: $125-$175**

Nickel-plated closed crescent with pierced 5-point star, "Deputy Marshal U.S." **Value: $100-$150**

Older badge assembled from parts of the Los Angeles Stamp & Stationery Co. 1900s circa style.
Value: $95-$125

Nickel-plated crescent 5-point star, "Deputy United States Marshal J.D. Morris." Personally owned badge used in the 1970s. **Value: $150-$175**

"Lieutenant American Protective League Auxilliary to U.S. Dept. of Justice." The A.P.L. existed from 1917-1919, helping various federal agencies track down internal enemies of the U.S.

Value: $175-$200

Total custom die eagle-top shield featuring draped enamel U.S. flags and coat-of-arms. Capitol Police Presidential Inaugural from 1989.

Value: $80-$100

Gold-plated custom die shield, "Federal Protective Service-General Services Administration Police 2196." FPS is responsible for policing buildings and grounds of the GSA.   **Value: $75-$100**

The second national issue style U.S. Marshal's badge, was used from 1970-1980. Sometimes referred to as the 'Patty Hearst' badge, as it was used during her arrest and trial.

Value: $375-$450

Custom die, gold-plated eagle-top sunburst shield, "1997 United States Capitol Police-Inauguration of the President of the United States."

Value: $80-$100

This collection includes badges of the U.S. Border Patrol and Immigration and Naturalization Service.

CHAPTER 9

MILITARY POLICE BADGES

When I refer to "military police," I mean the law enforcement branches of each of our five armed services: U.S. Army, U.S. Navy, U.S. Marines, U.S. Air Force and U.S. Coast Guard. The first military police were called, "Provost Marshals." The first Provost Marshal was appointed in 1776 and the Provost Corps operated during the Revolutionary War, War of 1812, and the Civil War. Provost Marshal badges were generally known to have been worn first during the Civil War. The Army Military Police Corps was established in 1919 and included a criminal investigation division. During the World Wars, military police usually wore cloth armbands that read, "MP." The duties of the MPs included combat with the regular infantry, and the armbands may or may not have been worn during these times. When guarding prisoners, providing base security, security for executive officers, and patrolling towns for GIs the MPs wore white helmets with the "MP" lettering as well as the armband. Since the inception of their

"U.S. Army Military Police Enid A.F.S.," (Air Force Station). Nickel-plated eagle-top shield with applied numbers in center. This 1940s shield shows wear on the numbers.
Value: $85-$120

use during the nineteenth century, military police badge styles varied considerably. These badges can be found with army base, fort, or division designations as a rule. Some read simply, "Military Police." The U.S. Army adopted a standard issue military police badge in 1975, which is still in use. These badges are a custom eagle top shield with a silver oxidized finish that read, "United States Army Military Police."

The second oldest military police would be the U.S. Coast Guard. The "Revenue Cutter Service" was established in 1790 to enforce customs laws. The Revenue Cutter Service and the Life-Saving Service was combined in 1915 into the United States Coast Guard (USCG). The USCG is charged with enforcing federal laws on the high seas and navigable waters in the U.S. The Intelligence and Law Enforcement Branch of the Coast Guard consists of "Special Agents" who are issued a custom shield badge with the USCG seal in the center as well as cloth badges or badge patches. Cutter personnel involved in law enforcement duties are called Tactical Law Enforcement Teams. Their uniform consists of a dark blue shirt and trousers with cloth badge and other cloth emblems.

The USCG, like all other branches, has security police personnel at stations and bases. USCG badges vary in design and are difficult to obtain because of the smaller size of the Coast Guard, thereby making them one of the more valuable military police badges.

The U.S. Air Force military police dates to 1948 when it was established under the Air Provost Marshal. Personnel were officially "Air Police," and wore a custom spread eagle top shield with USAF crest in center. The badge read, "Air Police-Department of the Air Force-United States of America." The center crest on early badges were enameled but later were silver that matched the rest of the badge. In 1967, the uniformed 'Air Police' was renamed, "Security Police." The same badge style was retained, only the wording was changed from "Air" to "Security." A reduced size version of the badge is also in use.

The uniformed police of the U.S. Navy are known as "Shore Patrolmen- SPs" which is usually a temporary assignment. The "Master-At-Arms," or "MAA" is the naval police on board ships as well as shore stations. A myriad of styles of MAA badges exist and are in use today. The symbol of the MAA is a shield with a circle 5-point star in the center.

This symbol is commonly seen as a center seal on MAA badges. Other center seals used include anchors, navy eagle, United States coat-of-arms, and plain 5-point stars. The navy issue MAA badge is 2-1/2 inches high with an eagle on top. It is a "catalog" badge except for the MAA symbol, or anchor, in the center which is in the badge's die. It is reverse stamped, raising the symbol's shape on the front of the badge. Navy badges will have a variety of wording which includes: MAA, Master-At-Arms, Police, Security Police, Chief MAA, Asst. Chief MAA, Base Patrolman, and will often designate a ship or naval base also. The back fasteners include pins, posts, and clutch backs.

The most recently formed military police is that of the U.S. Marine Corps. The first MP career field for Marines was established in 1968.

Prior to that, MP duties were temporary assignments as most other services had. A small variety of Marine MP badges have been used. The heart-shaped eagle top shield is the typical style. Wording is usually, "U.S. Marine Corps-Military Police - #," and will have the Marine Corps seal in the center. Recent issue badges are a light-weight badge, lettered the same way, except the lettering on the center seal reads, "United States Marine Corps-Law Enforcement" The more recent issue badges are difficult to obtain, but with some searching a collector should be able to find an older one.

Gold-plated eagle-top shield, "U.S. Marine Corps Military Police" with color seal, "United States Marine Corps Law Enforcement."

Value: $125-$150

U.S. Army World War II era eagle-top shield with U.S. disc in center. "Auxiliary Military Police 4."
Value: $75-$85

This eagle-top teardrop shield was made in the Philippines. "U.S. Navy ACMAA (Assistant Chief Master-At-Arms) Subic Bay." **Value: $35-$60**

The U.S. Army standardized their military police shields in the 1970s when they adopted this silver-oxidized custom eagle-top shield.
Value: $22-$30

"Patrolman Master at Arms USS Ranger 301." This nickel-plated shield shows hard use aboard the aircraft carrier Ranger. **Value: $45-$55**

U.S. Navy SMAA (Senior Master-At-Arms) USS
Midway CV-41.   **Value: $70-$80**

Modern Navy shield with MAA insignia stamped
into center of badge. "U.S. Navy MAA USS
New Jersey BB-62." "BB" is the designation for
a battleship.   **Value: $45-$60**

Another modern style Navy shield, this one with
stamped anchor in center. "U.S. Navy Police NAS
(Naval Air Station) Miramar."   **Value: $45-$60**

Current issue U.S. Air Force Security Police (left), reduced size version (center) and 1948-1967 issue, "Air Police" (right). **Value: $20-$25** **Value: $18-$22** **Value: $25-$35**

Nickel-plated sunburst shield, "Inspector Housing Office," with U.S. Coast Guard center seal. Rare.
Value: $125-$140

World War II era 6-point star with removed ball tips, "Police Petty Officer P.P.O. USS Intrepid CVA-11." "CV" is the designation for an aircraft carrier.
Value: $100-$125

Two-tone tear drop shield, "U.S. Marine Corps Military Police", with USMC seal. Sun Badge Hallmark.
Value: $130-$180

Nickel-plated eagle-top teardrop shield, "Security Patrolman Curtis Bay, Md. 8" with full-color enamel seal, "U.S. Coast Guard Yard." Rare.
Value: $175-$265

Some MAA badges are mounted to a leather holder so they can be fastened to a button on the uniform. "Master At Arms Naval Air Station NORIS," (North Island).
Value: $50-$65

CHAPTER 10

FOREIGN POLICE BADGES

I thought it would be helpful to include a chapter on badges from other countries as there have been a lot of them traded into the United States. I haven't tried to illustrate a badge from every foreign country, but I did want to show a good selection of those most commonly encountered. Generally speaking, most foreign badges are made of a lightweight, cheaper material than U.S. badges. However, some badges are quite handsome with their colorful enameling, like those from France.

Very few breast badges are used making most of the collectible badges, hat or helmet badges. Some collectors specialize in foreign badges, while many collectors have a representative collection including countries from which badges are easily obtained. The badges often don't have "police" marked on them, and many resemble military pieces. Value ranges on

Large size badge used on a 'Bobbie Helmet', called a "helmet plate." This one is from the West Yorkshire Constabulary, England.
Value: $10-$18

most foreign badges are quite low compared to American badges.

There are many somewhat obscure countries whose police insignia is quite difficult to obtain. In those cases, the collector must decide what it's worth to him to add the piece to his collection. Before Glasnost, Soviet police badges were almost impossible to obtain. Now they are easily found and still a popular badge with good variety.

Badges from the world famous "Royal Canadian Mounted Police" (RCMP) is a must for any badge collection. This organization was founded in 1873 as the "North West Mounted Police," and changed to the "Royal North West Mounted Police" in 1904, and then the "Royal Canadian Mounted Police" in 1920. A collector shouldn't have any problem finding the RCMP hat badge, but the 1873 and 1904 issues may be a little more difficult to locate.

Cap badges from England, "Oldham Police" (left), "Northumbria Police" (top), "Liverpool City Police" (right), and "West Yorkshire Constabulary" (bottom).

Value: $8-$15 ea.

French pocket and cap badges. Breast badges are worn on a leather holder which is fastened to a button on the tunic. **Value: $14-$22 ea.**

Top row, Australian cap badges; "Queensland Police," and "Western Australia Police."

Value: $30-$40 ea.

Lower left: "Tasmania Police" **Value: $30-$45**

Lower right: "New Zealand Police" helmet plate,

Value: $15-$18 ea.

This photo illustrates the difference in size between a British helmet plate and a cap badge.

Two nice representative badges of Canada, nickel-plated beaver-top shield with cut out numbers, "Police 3316 Montreal," and cap badge of the "Royal Canadian Mounted Police."

Value: $35-$55 ea.

A selection of police badges from Africa, starting top row left side, Libya, South Africa, Ghana, South Africa, Uganda, Bedfordview. **Value: $14-$18 ea.**

Two examples of larger size badges of France, the Gendarmerie, and National Police.

Value: $20-$30

Most cap badges of Germany resemble the shape of star-type badges. **Value: $8-$10 ea.**

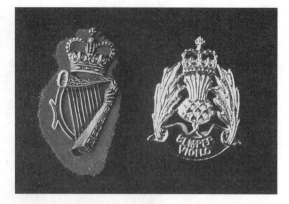

Hat badge of the Royal Ulster Constabulary of Northern Ireland (left), hat badge of the police of Scotland (right). **Value: $10-$15 ea.**

One example of many styles of police badges of the defunct Soviet Union. Before Glasnost, these items were very difficult to obtain. Hat badge and breast badge shown. **Value: $25-$30**

Top row left to right, Denmark, Norway. Bottom row left to right, Finland, Sweden. **Value: $12-$14 ea.**

Top left, Dutch State Police cap badge, right, cap badge of Italian police. Greek police badge on bottom. **Value: $12-$18 ea.**

CHAPTER 11

PATCHES: METHODS OF COLLECTING AND VALUATIONS

The embroidered emblem, uniform emblem, or patch is a piece of police insignia that came along much later than the metal badge. The process of embroidery, which is the art of stitching decorations on fabric or similar material with a needle and thread, has been used since ancient times.

Possibly one reason for its lateness in application to emblems is that police uniforms were not in heavy use until the mid to late nineteenth century. It would seem this type of insignia would lend itself better as further identification on a uniform than on civilian clothes. It should be noted that the U.S. military used embroidered rank insignia in the nineteenth century. Even at that, the uniform police patch didn't come into use until the 1930s and 1940s. Early patches were commonly made of felt with simple hand-embroidered lettering.

A popular but somewhat difficult state agency to collect is the Texas Department of Public Safety, which includes the Texas Rangers and Highway Patrol. Poor quality remakes and factory seconds have shown up on collectors tables. Shown are nine of the many divisions in the DPS. **Value: $4.50-$6.00**

Later, this type of embroidery was done on sewing machines, which helped somewhat with the appearance. Mass production patches made it possible to add designs and made lettering even and uniform. Today, patches are made on large computer-operated embroidery machines that can turn out colorful, high quality patches in large numbers in a relatively short time.

Methods of collecting patches are as diverse as badges with millions manufactured each year. Most law enforcement agencies in the U.S. use patches to help complete a professional looking uniform. As with badges, many collectors choose a topic or an area to collect. The following series of photos will illustrate numerous areas as well as provide basic value ranges.

A set of state game warden patches makes a sharp display, and yes, you can get all 50!
Value: $4.50-$5.50

Examples of early patches, some with hand-embroidered stars and lettering. Note unevenness of lettering compared to other early patches made by machine.   **Top row value: $4-$6**
Bottom row value: $8-15

Some modern departments prefer simple and less expensive designs like these sheriffs examples.
Value: $2.50-$3

Some of the lowest priced patches are those known as "stock" designs, which are made so that the department name can be added later.

Value: $2-$2.50

Motorcycle police patches are somewhat hard to find, and most of those are major cities. Shown are (top row left to right) New Orleans PD, New York City PD, Jersey City PD. (Bottom row) Rapides Parish, La. and Buffalo, N.Y. **Value: $3.75-$4.50**

It should be noted that reproductions are as prevalent in patches as they are in badges. Pictured on the left is a poor replica, on the right is the real thing. Regrettably, replicas can be of fine quality and almost impossible to detect. **Value: $3-$5**

In the last 10 years police bicycle units have become a very popular tool in Community Oriented Policing. Here are three examples of their patches. **Value: $4.00-$5.00**

Collecting all of the patches of a certain department is a popular area. The department may or may not be where the collector lives. Photo shows the regular shoulder patch of Philadelphia Police Dept., with only four of the many special unit patches this city uses.

Unit value: $3.50-$4.00
Regular patch value: $4.50-$5.00

Aviation units are a little harder to find, again it's usually major departments that have them.

Value: $4.50-$5.50

A selection of bomb squad patches from various cities. Many commonly share the U.S. Army explosives insignia as part of their design.

Value: $3-$4.50

The subdued colors of the special weapons teams, or SWAT teams as they are commonly called, make them readily identifiable. **Value: $3.50-$5**

Marine units are much lower in number as compared to K-9s. Large bodies of water obviously essential for the formation of such a unit.

Value: $5-$5.50

There are a lot of airports in the U.S. and most of any size have their own police agency. Here are examples of six 'airport police' patches.

Value: $3.50-$4.50

Another unit that is making a comeback in the 1980s & 1990s is the mounted unit.

Value: $5-$5.50

Also somewhat difficult patches to collect are those from railroad police agencies.

Value: $5-$8

Here's a collection of each state capitol's city police department.
Value: $3.50-$5.50

Police Honor Guards that have a special patch are somewhat hard to find. Most departments can organize a squad to serve as an Honor Guard, but have no special patch. **Value: $5-$6**

A fun and educational collection is compiled with patches from famous places, or places known for a special person or thing. Shown (top row R to L) Salem, MA, Kingfisher, OK, Kill Devil Hills, NC, Storey CO, Virginia City, NV, Tombstone, AZ, Dodge City, KS, and Lawrenceburg, TN. **Value: $3.50-$6**

A very popular area to collect is that of the Indian tribal police. These handsome patches often have Indian symbolism that makes them very attractive. **Value: $6-$8**

Police pistol competitions usually have patches available, and may be most popular with the partici-pants. **Value: $3-$4.50**

Certain states are popular collecting areas such as Alaska and Hawaii. Shown is a selection of colorful Alaskan police patches. **Value: $5-$10**

Although security patches, like badges do not hold a similar value to regular law enforcement insignia. A minimal collection should consist of the old major companies as shown. **Value: $3-$4**

A selection of Hawaiian police patches, which are fewer in number, but just as popular.
Value: $4-$8

Unfortunately the large size of some departments make their patches very common in the hobby and thereby reduce their worth. **Value: $2-$2.50**

CHAPTER 12

POLICE AND SHERIFF PATCHES

The most plentiful patches available are from city police and county sheriffs' departments. This is simply because there are more of these agencies than any other. The variety of styles is wide, as are the prices. Many dealers offer large selections which are good sources for trade stock and additions to your collections. A person should be aware of a few things when buying from these dealers.

A selection of modern police patches from around the country.
Value: $3.50-$4.50

Avoid dealers who ask premium prices. As stated previously, there are a lot of patches available from many dealers and collectors. Most patches, when ordered in a quantity of 100 or more, rarely cost more than $2 to $4 each. A patch that has full embroidery coverage will cost more than one with only 30% embroidery coverage. Difficulty in obtaining certain patches will obviously add to their value. A New York City police patch is one of the most common, but patches from a now defunct department are usually harder to find.

They may not be the actual source for the agency's patches that they handle. Some dealers send an authentic patch to a manufacturer and order a quantity of them, for sales "stock." These patches technically couldn't be called authentic, however, sometimes this is the only way you can obtain certain patches. It's up to the individual collector if he/she has a problem with this. Some dealers carry "seconds," which are patches that have defects in the embroidery, or feature incorrect colors, etc. These have no place in a collection. There are too many good patches available to be purchasing defects.

Twenty years ago it wasn't uncommon to be able to write to an agency to obtain their patch for free, or be able to purchase their patch. Today, your best chance is when writing, is to contact a collector in the department who can sell or trade his patch. Tight budgets of today's agencies don't allow patches to be sent out for free. Some agencies maintain a display and will trade for your patch. The hobby has increased in size tremendously over the past 10 to 15 years, and collectors

139

don't realize how many requests police and sheriffs departments receive.

It wouldn't be practical to list every police department in the U.S., but for those collecting county patches, here is a list indicating the number of counties in each state:

Alabama 67

Alaska 16
  (6 independent boroughs, 10 covered by state troopers)

Arizona 15

Arkansas 75

California 58

Colorado 63

Connecticut ...8

Delaware 3

Florida 67

Georgia 159

Hawaii 5

Idaho 44

Illinois............102

Indiana...........92

Iowa 99

Kansas............105

Kentucky 120

Louisiana........64
  (parishes)

Maine 16

Maryland 23
  (1 city)

Massachusetts.14

Michigan........83

Minnesota......87

Mississippi 82

Missouri.........114
  (1 city)

Montana 56

Nebraska 93

Nevada...........16
  (1 city)

New Hampshire......10

New Jersey 21

New Mexico...33

New York 62
  (1 city)

North Carolina..........100

North Dakota 53

Ohio 88

Oklahoma 77

Oregon...........36

Pennsylvania...67

Rhode Island ..5

South Carolina 46

South Dakota .66

Tennessee 95

Texas 254

Utah...............29

Vermont.........14

Virginia..........95
  (40 cities)

Washington....39

West Virginia .55

Wisconsin 72

Wyoming 23

Many collectors prefer brand new patches that have never been sewn onto a uniform, and will often reject trades involving used patches. This contradicts the badge collecting ideology that badges which have been used, and preferably show honest wear, are the best. Used patches, in good displayable condition offer just as much character as a worn badge. An item actually used in service is always a worthwhile collectible. **Value: $2-$3**

Many police and sheriff's departments have adopted colorful designs that reflect the history or symbolism of their jurisdiction. **Value: $4.50-$5.50**

A selection of modern sheriff patches from around the country. **Value: $3.50-$4.50**

CHAPTER 13

STATE POLICE AND HIGHWAY PATROL PATCHES

There are 49 state police/highway patrol (SP/HP) agencies in the United States. This is a set of patches most collectors complete at one time or another. There are only 49 agencies, as Hawaii has no state police. Hobbyists who want to represent Hawaii in their state collection, use the Hawaii Public Safety-State Sheriff patch.

Over the past several years, a large number of "special unit" patches (bomb squad, K-9, emergency vehicle operations, aviation, tactical, marine, etc.) have appeared in use by SP/HP agencies. Most, but not all of these, are official patches. If a person opens his/her SP/HP collecting to all types of patches, there exists a virtual endless list available. In addition to the

In addition to the regular issue shoulder patches, state patrol agencies have many 'unit' patches which are highly collectable.
Value: $3.50-$5.50

special units, many agencies have had anniversaries (50 years, 60 years, etc.) and had commemorative patches made.

Some states have made their patches available for purchase through trooper associations. This is good for collectors, because it assures that they get an authentic patch. Remember, many dealers and mail order police suppliers stock all 49 SP/HP patches and they all can't be the agencies' supplier!

In addition, many of these departments have gone through re-organization which resulted in name changes. Obsolete, or old-style patches are getting somewhat difficult to find, due to age and the popularity of collecting SP/HP.

The Internet is a great source for information and addresses in all areas of law enforcement collecting.

CHAPTER 14

FEDERAL AGENCY PATCHES

The collecting of federal law enforcement patches is much more relaxed than the area of federal badges, even though technically the U.S. Code includes all insignia (refer to Chapter 8). As one might expect, there exists a large array of patches in this area. Again, the collector should be aware that not all are official patches. For those that collect only agency issued patches, this will be a problem. Many, however, collect all federal patches whether they

Top patch: U.S. Marshal's Service Seal, Western District of Michigan, District of Maryland, and regular issue jacket patch.   Value: $5-$7

are officially authorized by the agency or not. It's difficult to know if it is really official, and to find out for sure would take a call to that agency. Corresponding with well-known collectors would be a better bet.

A partial list of Federal Police Agencies is given in Chapter 8, so that won't be repeated here. For the benefit of newer collectors, the following list identifies a small number of the federal patches that are available.

- Training Academy United States Secret Service
- United States Secret Service Police Revolver Team
- Executive Protective Service United States Secret Service Academy
- Treasury Police United States Secret Service
- U.S. Dept. of Interior Bureau of Indian Affairs Marijuana Reconnaissance Eradication Team
- Drug Enforcement Administration 20 Years 1973-1993
- Customs High Endurance Tracker United States Customs Service Miami Air Branch
- U.S. Customs Buffalo Contraband Enforcement Team
- Bayou Bushwackers U.S. Customs New Orleans, LA
- U.S. Border Patrol Air Operations
- First Responder Unit United States Capitol Police
- United States Treasury Department Smurfbusters
- National Forensic Lab Criminal Investigation U.S. Treasury
- Boston FBI SWAT
- Los Angeles FBI Swat
- FBI Academy—The Rule of Law, Not Men
- FBI National Academy
- FBI Investigative Support Unit
- FBI SWAT Detroit
- FBI Hostage Negotiator
- New York FBI
- FBI ABSCAM Surveillance Team
- FBI Boston Dept. of Justice
- Philadelphia FBI SWAT
- FBI Electronics Technician
- FBI SWAT Team Norfolk Div.
- FBI Washington, D.C. BCCI Squad
- FBI New Haven SWAT
- FBI New York Office SWAT
- FBI Washington Metropolitan Field Office
- Ashland, KY RA (resident agent) FBI
- United States Marshal Bicentennial 1789-1989

- United States Marshal Wyoming
- United States Marshal Nebraska
- Operation Trident Southern District Ohio Columbus Ohio U.S. Marshal
- U.S. Marshal's Service Operation Trident '93
- U.S. Marshal Special Operation Group Missile Escort
- U.S. Marshal's Service National Prisoner Transportation System Dept. of Justice
- U.S. Marshal District Maryland
- Dept. of Justice U.S. Marshal Western District Michigan
- U.S. Marshal's Service Operation Hagar
- U.S. Marshal's Service Operation Gunsmoke NY
- U.S. Marshal's Service Operation Sunrise Fugitive Apprehension Squad
- Middle District Pennsylvania U.S. Marshal
- U.S. Marshal's Posse Western District Texas
- U.S. Marshal's Posse NY
- U.S. Marshal W. Dist. NY
- U.S. Marshal N. Dist. Oklahoma
- U.S. Marshal E. Dist. Pennsylvania

A small selection of patches of the Federal Bureau of Investigation. Top row: FBI seals, middle row, FBI Office Boston, FBI Philadelphia SWAT, FBI SWAT Team Norfolk Division. Bottom row: FBI Hostage Negotiator, FBI National Academy, FBI Washington Field Office. **Value: $4.50-$7**

Federal patches from the Federal Protective Service, F.A.A. Police, Fed. Law Enforcement Training Center, Arlington National Cemetery, Treasury/A.T.F., Dept. of Justice, National Park Service, U.S. Postal Police, Veteran's Administration Police.   **Value: $4-$5.50**

Federal patches: Bureau of Engraving and Printing Police, Amtrak Police, Drug Enforcement Administration, U.S. Customs, U.S. Border Patrol, Dept. of Defense, U.S. Capitol Police, U.S. Embassy Guard, Smithsonian Institution, Dept. of Agriculture, and the Food and Drug Administration.

Value: $4.50-$5.50

Federal patches: Hoover Dam Police, Bureau of Reclamation Police, National Zoological Park Police, U.S. Fish & Wildlife Service, National Institutes of Health Police, Kennedy Space Center Security, Enviromental Protection Agency Special Agent, U.S. Supreme Court Police, U.S. Govt. Printing Office, U.S. Forest Service, Dept. of Justice Bureau of Prisons, Dept. of State Special Agent.

Value: $4-$5.50

Like badges, federal patches are a popular item to collect. It is amazing the number a federal police agencies their are, and the diversity of their insignia. Shown are patches from the U.S. Secret Service, Immigration, Bureau of Indian Affairs, U.S. Park Police, U.S. Treasury and Mint.   **Value: $4.50-$8**

The United States Marshal's Service has a wide variety of official and non-official patches including District patches, special duty patches and commemorative patches.   **Value: $4.50-$8**

In 1989, the U. S. Marshal's Service celebrated their 200th anniversary. Many districts had special patches made for this occasion. Shown are three examples: Bicentennial badge style, District of Nebraska, District of Wyoming.   **Value: $5-$7**

CHAPTER 15

MILITARY POLICE PATCHES

Military police
patches are another varied
area of collecting. When
starting out, one may
want to obtain standard
uniform insignias which
are usually available from
dealers
in militaria.

The uniform insignia
from the U.S. Army
would include the differ-
ent M.P. brigades such as
the 15th, 18th, 43rd, 220th, 221st, 290th, and
300th M.P. Brigade. The U.S. Army Criminal
Investigation Command patch fits here also.
Miscellaneous patches include K-9 Corps, Auxiliary MP (WWII), Investigator, etc. The Army
MP armband is also an interesting addition to the
collection. These have been made of different
materials through the years such as felt and vinyl,
usually in black, but also found in OD green with
black letters. Some armbands may be found with
unit or division patches attached.

The Air Force has a large number of "Security Police Squadron" and old style, "Air Police"
patches available. The obsolete "AP" (Air Police)
armbands are getting somewhat difficult to
locate, but they are a nice addition.

The U.S. Navy has 3rd, 2nd, and 1st class
petty officer rates (type of rank chevrons) that

Examples of U.S. Air Force Air/Security Police
patches, some subdued and some in color.
Value: $3-$4.50

include the "Master-at-
Arms" MAA (police)
emblem. There is also a
MAA badge patch in use.
Various naval bases have
security police patches,
some are Navy, and some
are Dept. of Defense
Guards. Again, armbands
marked with "SP" (Shore
Patrol) make a collection
more complete.

The Marine Corps
uses an armband also, but it is red with
yellow/gold letters, "MP." Miscellaneous patches
may include, K-9, and drug detection.

The U.S. Coast Guard (USCG) has a lot of
different types of patches, all of which technically
could be included here, as it's a federal maritime
law enforcement agency. Included in this wide
area are patches for cutters (ships), bases, air
stations, groups, training centers, districts, marine
safety offices, search and rescue, as well as law
enforcement. Like the Navy, the USCG has rates
with the symbol of the "Port Securityman",
and the old-style "G" for guard. Other interesting law enforcement (LE) patches include badge
patches for the Coast Guard Special Agents, LE
detachments, boarding officer (patches and
armbands), the tactical LE teams, as well as base
security police.

CHAPTER 16

FOREIGN POLICE PATCHES

Collecting foreign insignia is a large field of its own. Luckily, there are a multitude of foreign collectors who are very devoted to the hobby and are happy to trade with Americans. The greatest number of collectors seem to be located in Germany, Great Britain, France, Australia, and New Zealand. There are collectors worldwide, and through these contacts, a collector should be able to build a respectable display.

Some patches from Australia's neighbor, New Zealand.
Value: $4-$5.50

Like badges, foreign patches sometimes do not say "police" on them, not in English anyway! One should take note of how the word "police" appears on some of these foreign patches.

The largest variety of patches undoubtedly comes from Germany, and the fewest come from Great Britain. There are many colorful and interesting patches from around the world, and with our foreign country relationships improving, it's a great time to build a collection.

Country	Word for police
Switzerland and Germany	Polizei
Spain and Mexico	Policia
Denmark and Norway	Politi
Sweden	Polis
Netherlands and Belgium	Politie

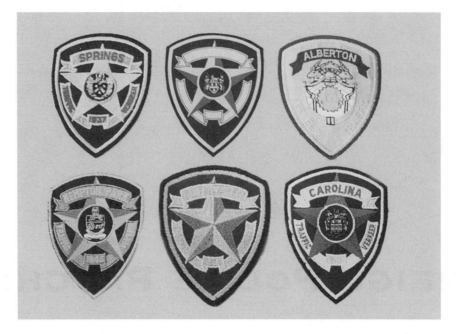

South African Police patches, Springs, Johannesburg, Alberton, Kempton Park, Bethlehem and Carolina. **Value: $4.50-$6**

Patches of the Netherlands, State Police on top, and City Police on bottom. **Value: $3.50-$4.50**

Scandinavian countries, upper left Norway, below Denmark, center Sweden and right Finland. **Value: $3.50-$4.50**

Various West German police agencies.
Value: $3-$4.50

French National and municipal police emblems.
Value: $4-$4.50

Mexican city police on right and left, with Federal police in center, current on top and old style on bottom. **Value: $4.50-$5**

Assorted foreign patches, top row L to R; Switzerland, Thailand, Spain, bottom row L to R; Italy, Austria, Philippines and Brunei.
Value: $5-$6.50

Canadian patches including the Royal Canadian Mounted Police, Ontario Provincial Police (O.P.P.) and various city police forces.
Value: $3.50-$4.50

Some patches of Australia, top row L to R: New South Wales Sheriff, New South Wales Police, Australian Capital Territory Police. Bottom row L to R: Victoria Police, Australian Federal Police, South Australia Police and Australian Customs.
Value: $5.50-$6.00

Aboriginal patches of Australia are somewhat hard to find and demand a higher price due to the small agencies involved. **Value: $12-$18**

CHAPTER 17

MINIATURE POLICE VEHICLES

Collecting miniature police vehicles has become one of the most popular and fastest growing segments of the hobby today. The sheer number that have been released in the last five years alone, preclude them from all being illustrated here. For the purposes of this work, I am primarily talking about modern made die-cast metal vehicles and plastic model kits.

Some of the commonly found die-casts are made by Matchbox, Hot Wheels, Corgi, Majorette, Ertl, Eligor, Vitesse, Rextoys and Road Champs. Some are available separately and some come in sets. Sizes range from 1/64 to 1/25 scale. The 1/64 scale are very popular, as are the various 1/43 scale cars. Examples differ in authenticity of vehicle type as well as markings. Some of those that offer realistic vehicles and markings are the 1/43 scale Road Champs. Their first line of state police cars was offered in 1993. Since then, they have expanded the state police line to also include city and park police, capital city police and sport utility trucks in police markings. Road Champs has continually added new models to their line

Ertl, 1940 Ford Woody. (1/43)   **Value: $10-$12**

which almost immediately dates any comprehensive list. Liberty Classics Inc. has released a line of 1/25 scale vintage police vehicles which feature authentic vehicles and markings, right down to the license plates!

Plastic model kit manufacturers more or less ignored the police car market until the 1980s. Most of the police kits that were released prior to this time were in a hot rod or show car mode, with the exception of two kits offered by Jo-Han Models Inc., which were a 1960 Plymouth station wagon and a 1968 Plymouth Fury 4-door sedan. The '60 Plymouth came with only one generic style of decals but the '68 came with a variety of accurately done major city decals. Both kits came with police equipment that would authentically outfit them. Another police car kit of the time worth mentioning was AMT's 1970 Ford Interceptor Police 4-door sedan. This kit came with Troy, Michigan Police markings and equipment. In the late 70s, we also saw two Dodge police kits offered, both by MPC. First was the 1977 Dodge Monaco 2-door Force 440 Police Pursuit Vehicle, which included a nice array of police equipment including small arms. The next MPC release was a replica of Sheriff Roscoe's cruiser from the TV show, *The Dukes of Hazzard*. This was the '77 Dodge but with 4-doors, and was welcomed by those who built police models. This timeless kit has been released a total of three different times.

The second release was another TV car, this time a replica from *T.J. Hooker*. In 1989, the third time it was released, it had the make-up of a Gotham City Police car from the movie, *Batman* or could be constructed as a goon car. The 1980s also produced a nice 1/32 scale Chevy Malibu Police car under the Monogram banner.

The 1990s started out with a bang for the hobby when AMT/Ertl released the much anticipated '90 Taurus Police kit. The kit came with California Highway Patrol markings and modern light bar. It was also released three different times, the second being the Taurus Police from the movie, RoboCop 2, and the third time as a cruiser from the Emergency 911 TV show. Lindberg has decided they too would produce something for the police car market, and started with a 1/20 scale Texas Highway Patrol Camaro; and they have also added a California Highway Patrol Camaro and Ford Explorer.

In all probability, there never was a more anticipated kit than the 1/25 scale Revell '91 Chevrolet Caprice police car. It came with an oversized electronic light bar as well as an accurate display unit. The police car hobby clamored for more, but the manufacturers sat by and watched the market. Finally in 1997, Lindberg released their 1/25 scale Ford Crown Victoria equipped with Ohio State Highway Patrol markings, which hit the target audience dead on. The kit is equipped with a state-of-the-art light bar and accurate markings. The miniature police vehicle hobby just continues to grow and improve!

Die-cast Vehicles

The Road Champs series started in 1993. The vehicles are marked with the year of manufacture either on the bottom or on rear license plate. Here is a value guide and list current at this time:

Original retail prices	$3.29-$4.00 range.
1993 Series	$15-$25
1994 Series	$10-$12
1995, 96, 97	$6-$8

State Police, City & Park Police:

Washington, Michigan, Denver, CO
Idaho, Minnesota, Las Vegas, NV
Texas, New Jersey, Columbus, OH
Alaska, Ohio, Atlanta, GA
Ohio 1933-1993, Nashville, TN
W. Virginia, Florida, Tallahassee, FL
Colorado, Missouri, Trenton, NJ
Vermont, Louisiana, Wash. D.C.
Maine, California, Chicago, IL
Wyoming, Rhode Island, Chicago, IL COPS
Mississippi, Kansas, Orlando, FL
Alabama, Maryland, Lancaster, PA
New Mexico, Indiana, Anaheim, CA
Arizona, Oregon-white, Annapolis, MD
Nevada, Oregon-black & white, Augusta, ME
Georgia-Chev, South Carolina, Columbia, SC
Georgia-Ford, Oklahoma, Des Moines, IA
Utah, North Carolina, Hartford, CT
Tennessee, Montana, Helena, MT
North Dakota, Iowa, Indianapolis, IN
South Dakota, Massachusetts, Jackson, MS
Nebraska, Puerto Rico, New Orleans, LA
Illinois, Kentucky, Sacramento, CA
Arkansas, Salt Lake City, UT
Virginia, Springfield, IL
New York error color, Branson, MO
New York, Port Authority of NY/NJ
Wisconsin, Louisville, KY
Savannah, GA
Gettysburg, PA
North Pole, AK
Royal Canadian Mounted Police Topeka, KS
Ontario Provincial Police Baton Rouge, LA
Quebec Provincial Police Phoenix, AZ
Niagara Regional Police Little Rock, AR
Vancouver, B.C. Police Boise City, ID
Montreal Police Lincoln, NE
Niagara Falls, Ont. Police Charleston, WV

Light Duty Trucks:

New Jersey Suburban
Rhode Island Suburban
Nevada Suburban
Wash. DC Blazer
W. Virginia Cherokee

"Premier" editions of Road Champs are limited editions specially ordered by the police agencies or organizations. Prices run from $10+.

Matchbox has joined in with a set of limited edition police cars. These cars are from their standard line, but are highly-detailed including accurate paint and markings. Their production is "limited" like this New Jersey State Police Ltd. and Virginia State Police Ltd.   **Value: $12-$18**

A 1917 Ford Model T paddy wagon bank, made by Ertl, released by Signed With Pride Die Cast Collectibles.   **Value: $35-$40**

1905 paddy wagon bank by Signed With Pride Die Cast Collectibles.   **Value: $18-$24**

An Ertl 1905 Ford Model T police van bank This was 1st in a series by the Phoenix Exchange.
Value: $18-$24

This outstanding 1949 Mercury Police car by the Danbury Mint in 1/24 scale features opening doors, hood, trunk and front wheels that turn by operating the steering wheel. Other details include police radio, spotlight, red roof light plus an officer's jacket and nightstick laying on the front seat. Generic police decals mark the doors.

Value: $115-$125

Rextoys created a line of 1935 Fords: black & white Montana Highway Patrol coupe (shown), all white Nassau Co. N.Y. Police coupe, and a black & gray Los Angeles, CA. Police four-door sedan. All in 1/43 scale.   **Value: $18-$22ea.**

Touring car marked "Police" by Lledo from their Days Gone series.   **Value: $6-$8**

Another Rextoys creation, a 1935 Chrysler Airflow, Indiana State Police, 1/43 scale.   **Value: $18-$22**

1946 Chrysler by Vitesse, 1/43 scale police.   **Value: $18-$22**

A 1962 Corvair from Eligor with generic police markings.   **Value: $8-$10**

Matchbox Super Kings, late 1970s Plymouths. Many police vehicles have been Grand Fury police cars, 1/43 scale.   **Value: $8-$12 ea.**

A series of three Soviet police (militia) vehicles. Manufactured in the U.S.S.R.
Value: $20-$25 ea.

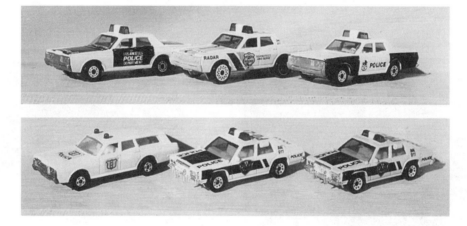

Matchbox 1968 Mercurys and 80s Ford Crown Victorias. Mercurys   **Value $3-$4 ea.**
Crown Victorias   **Value: $1.50-$2 ea.**

A 1950s model police car kit, manufactured by the Ideal Co., representing the police car from the TV program "Dragnet." This kit is in unbuilt mint condition and a fine collectible.   **Value: $125-$150**

Note: Kit values are based on unbuilt MIB condition.

The JO-Han 1968 Plymouth Police Pursuit Car. (1/25)   **Value: $20-$25**

MPC Police Trail Patrol Truck. (1/32) **Value: $4-$5**

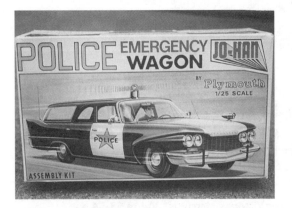

The JO-Han 1960 Plymouth Emergency Wagon. (1/25)   **Value: $15-$18**

Revell Z-28 Police Car. (1/25) This kit featured a non-stock body.   **Value: $4-$5**

AMT 1970 Ford Interceptor Police Car. (1/25)   **Value: $20-$30**

Hobby Heaven re-release.   **Value: $15-$18**

Revell SWAT Command Van. (1/32) **Value: $6-$8**

MPC Police Patrol Car 1949 Mercury. (1/25)
Value: $12-$15

AMT/ERTL Joker Goon Car/Gotham City Police
Car. (1/25)   **Value: $12-$15**

MPC Force 440 Police Pursuit Vehicle. (1/25)
Value: $25-$30

Monogram Chevy Police Car. (1/32) **Value: $5-$6**

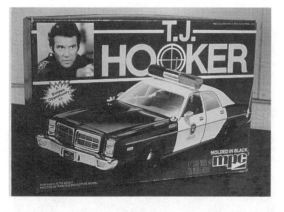

MPC T.J. Hooker Police car. (1/25) **Value: $18-$25**

AMT/ERTL Taurus Police Car. (1/25)
Value: $10-$15

AMT/ERTL ROBO 1 Police Car. (1/25)
Value: $12-$16

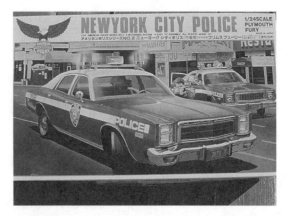

YODEL New York City Police. (1/24)
Value: $18-$22

AMT/ERTL Rescue 911 Police Car. (1/25)
Value: $6-$8

YODEL New York/New Jersey Port Authority
Police. (1/24) **Value: $18-$22**

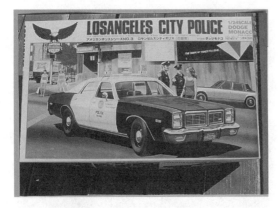

YODEL Los Angeles City Police. (1/24)
Value: $18-$22

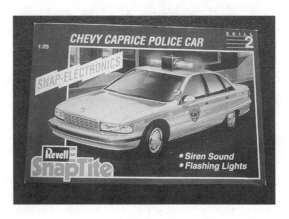

Revell Chevy Caprice Police Car. (1/25)
Value: $12-$14

Revell C.H.i.Ps Kawasaki 1000. (1/12)
Value: $20-$25

Note: Also in the series, but not shown, are a James B. Beam Distilling Co. Police Decanter Ford V-8 Tow Truck (#3 in series), value: $135-$140; 1934 Ford Police Patrol Car (#4 in series), value: $130-$135; Chevy State Trooper Car (#5 in series & last), value: $110-$120.

1940 Ford sedan, California Highway Patrol. (Liberty Set #1)   **Value: $25-$35**

James B. Beam Distilling Co. Police Decanter 1929 Ford Model A Police (#1 in series-1982).
Value: $150-$155

This 1932 Ford paddy wagon also made by Eligor. 1/43 scale.   **Value: $12-$17**

James B. Beam Distilling Co. Police Decanter 1931 Ford AA Paddy Wagon (#2 in series).
Value: $145-$150

1936 Dodge Panel Delivery, Chicago Police Dept. (Liberty Set #1)
Value: $25-$35

Three examples of the popular 1/43 scale Road Champs cars, (lor) New
Orleans Police, Royal Canadian Mounted Police, and the Idaho State
Police. **Value: $10-$25**

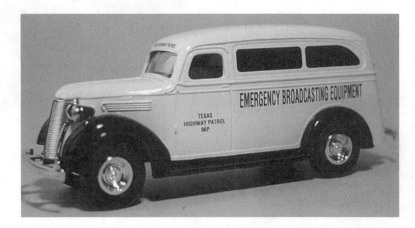

The Ertl Co. has a line of 1/43 and 1/25 scale vehicles. The 1/25 scale vehicles are banks like this 1938 Chevy Texas Highway Patrol van.
Value: $25-$30

An outstanding quality line of vintage 1/25 scale die-cast police vehicles was released in 1998, by Liberty Classics, Inc. of Libertyville, IL. Known for automotive advertising banks, Liberty's new, "Law Enforcement" series is a limited edition collector's series of non-banks. Based on vehicles from the early teens to the 1950s, the color and markings are carefully researched, to produce the most authentic cars and trucks possible. Each vehicle in the series comes with miniature insignia of the department represented. They are released from the company, three at a time. The "Law Enforcement" series is available at the larger chain stores, hobby shops, and mail order companies.

1940 Ford Convertible, Ohio State Highway Patrol
(Liberty Set #2)   **Value: $25-$30**

1955 Chevrolet sedan Delivery, Philadelphia Police Dept.
(Liberty Set #2)   **Value: $25-$30**

1948 Ford Panel, Denver Police Dept.
(Liberty Set #3)   **Value: $25-$30**

A finely done 1941 Chevrolet, Michigan State Police
in 1/43 by Durham Automotive Miniatures. Markings are correct for the era represented.
Value: $75-$100

1931 Ford Model A roadster, Missouri State Highway Patrol (Liberty Set #3)   **Value: $20-$30**

Road Champs, New Jersey Suburban, West Virginia
Cherokee, and Wash. D.C. Blazer.
Value: $10-$15

CHAPTER 18

LICENSE PLATES

The police license plate can be considered one of the first markings on patrol cars starting in the 1920s and 1930s. Often the plate alone would identify the plain black sedan or roadster. Most often it was the state police and highway patrol agencies that had unique plates that had the department's name on them. Larger city agencies also used unique plates.

For collecting purposes, the most valuable plates are those early marked plates which are far

New Hampshire Dept. of Safety (State Police).
Value: $25-$30

and few between today. Since the 1940s and 1950s most state police agencies use custom plates and many other departments followed suit. Plates that are in excellent condition, with agency name on it, are the most sought after.

There were and still are many jurisdictions that issue plates marked only with, "municipal," "county," "city," "government," or "official." These are worth far less than custom plates.

Alabama State Trooper plate.   **Value: $25-$30**

North Carolina (HP) Highway Patrol plate.
Value: $20-$25

Maryland State Police plate.   **Value: $15-$20**

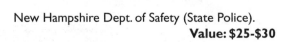

New Hampshire Dept. of Safety (State Police).
Value: $25-$30

Patrol license plate display at the Missouri State Highway
Patrol museum in Jefferson City.

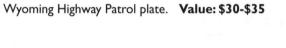

Wyoming Highway Patrol plate.   **Value: $30-$35**

Columbia Mo. Police plate.   **Value: $25-$30**

Wisconsin Official State Patrol (slightly damaged).
Value: $15-$20

Nebraska City Govt.; Nebraska Government.
Value: $10-$12ea.

CHAPTER 19

BILLY CLUBS & NIGHTSTICKS

The billy club has been an integral part of the policeman's equipment since the 1800s. Manufactured of several different kinds of hardwoods the 'billy' usually measured anywhere from 6" to 8" and could be carried in a special narrow pocket made in the uniform coat or trousers.

The nightstick, longer than the billy got its name from use by night patrolmen who not only used the stick to control unruly suspects, but used it as a means of communication with other patrolmen. A certain number of raps on the street would bring help at a run. The riot baton is thicker

From left to right:
Wooden nightstick   **Value: $10-$15**
Wooden billy club   **Value: $8-$10**
Modern hard plastic club **Value: $5-$8**
Modern short billy   **Value: $3-$5**

and much longer than the nightstick and is issued only for emergency riot control duties.

Modern nightsticks and billys are made of modern materials such as hard plastics, rubber and aluminum. These have minimum collector's interest.

The most sought after are the hardwood sticks dating around the turn of the century. Some had department names or the officer's name carved into them. The most valuable of all are those custom made especially for presentation purposes. These can be near priceless pieces adorned with handles made of ivory carvings. A very rare police collectible indeed!

CHAPTER 20

UNIFORMS AND CAPS

Major American cities adopted uniforms for their police forces by the mid-nineteenth century. Post civil war photographs show some military uniforms were even pressed into service. Colors for the early uniforms were usually blue with some departments using gray. Eventually, blue won out as the national color for police agencies. Unfortunately, the survival rate for these nineteenth century uniforms is fairly low, and so they would bring top dollar in displayable condition.

When I talk about collectable uniforms, I mean a uniform (new or old) that is complete with all badges, collar insignia, shoulder patches, hat with badge and trousers. Some collectors demand the uniform to be

City of New York Police Mounted Unit tunic complete with badge. **Value: $130-$140**

complete down to the duty leather and footwear. The value of a uniform shirt with nothing but shoulder patches affixed is minimal. To fully enjoy uniforms they should be displayed, wherein lies one drawback of this collectable and that is space.

Mannequins decked out in full uniforms make a very nice display, but they do take up a lot of room. More often than not, these items get stuck on hangers and stored in a closet. Because of this problem, some collectors choose to collect only caps, which don't take up as much room.

The following photos are a small sampling of caps and uniforms that are in use around the world.

Cap, State Police, the Netherlands.
Value: $30-$40

Missouri State Highway Patrol felt campaign hat.
Value: $50-$65

State Police, The Netherlands complete with duty belt.
Value: $135-$150

West German Police cap.
Value: $22-$28

City of New York Police cap.
Value: $25-$35

Royal Ulster Constabulary-Ireland cap.
Value: $30-$40

Spanish Civil Guard tricorne hat. **Value: $65-$70**

New South Wales Police, Australia.
Value: $45-$60

Belgian Police cap. **Value: $25-$30**

Italian Carabinieri cap. **Value: $30-$40**

City Police, The Netherlands cap. **Value: $25-$30**

French Police kepi. **Value: $35-$45**

Metropolitan Police, London, England "bobby helmet." **Value: $95-$115**

Nottinghamshire Constabulary, England "bobby helmet." **Value: $95-$115**

CHAPTER 21

RESTRAINTS

Handcuffs and leg irons were first mass produced in the mid-1800s by many manufacturers. Imports, especially from Great Britain came into common use in the U.S. also.

Because of the great extent and variety of this collecting area, the best information to pass along to collectors is to make yourself familiar with

Handcuffs, "Made in USA, Marcas Registradas, Smith & Wesson, Springfield, Mass."   **Value: $25-$35**

prices from antiques catalogs, sale flyers, and from trusted dealers in police antiquities.

The market for restraints fluctuates so much, it makes assembling a price guide risky business. The accompanying photos serve to only illustrate a small assortment of what is available to collectors today. Prices are very general.

Tower (U.S.) handcuffs, patented 1874.
Value: $110-$150

Leg irons, "American Munitions Company, Chicago, Il." 1940s. **Value: $175-$190**

Turn-of-the-century British Hiatt's handcuffs, with screw key. **Value: $120-$145**

Bean Cobb leg irons, 1909. **Value: $200-$275**

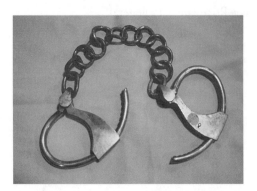

Tower Double Lock (U.S.) leg irons, late 1800s.
Value: $190-$220

Handcuffs, nineteenth century. **Value: $150-$200**

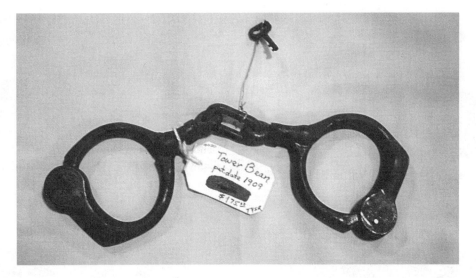

Tower Bean, handcuffs, 1909.   **Value: $150-$175**

Harvard Lock Co. handcuffs.   **Value: $45-$65**

Malcolm Co. Claw come-along, 1912.
                              Value: $350-$395

Hiatt's chrome-plated handcuffs.
                    Value: $140-$165

Claw come-along.   **Value: $120-$140**

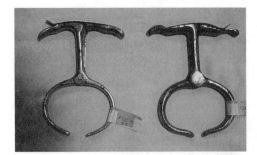

Come-alongs.　　　　　　　　**Value: $110-$135**

Handcuffs, "Stoeger-New York, Chief of Police-Zephyr Police."　　　　**Value: $25-$35**

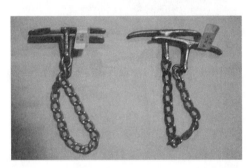

Come-alongs, sometimes called "chain twisters."
Value: $120-$140

Handcuffs, "Star-Made in Spain."　**Value: $20-$25**

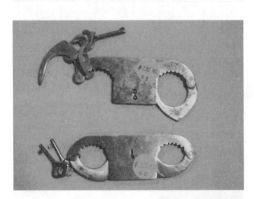

Thumb cuffs.　　　　　　**Value: $120-$140**
.　　　　　　　　　　　**Value: $500-$750**

Handcuffs, "The Peerless Handcuff Co. Springfield, Mass."　　　　　　　**Value: $25-$35**

Handcuffs, "Colt's Pt. F.A. Mfg. Co. Hartford, CT. U.S.A."　　　　　　**Value: $75-$90**

CHAPTER 22

BOOKS AND PAPER ITEMS

There exists an unlimited number of paper collectibles containing a police motif. A collector would indeed be kept busy collecting everything in an area of this type. This chapter is meant to give a sampling of some of those items that can be found.

The FBI Story. 1963.   **Value: $8-$10**

FBI-The G-Men's Weapons and Tactics for Combating Crime. 1954.   **Value: $6-$8**

Men Against Crime 1946.   **Value: $5-$7**
Behind the Silver Shield 1946.   **Value: $5-$7**

Juvenile books on the police.
Let's Go to a Police Station. 1957.   **Value: $4-$6**
On the Beat Policemen at Work. 1968.   **Value: $4-$6**

Annual Report Board of Police Justices City of New York
1886.   **Value: $55-$65**

The Royal Canadian Mounted Police 1873-1987.
1988.   **Value: $8-$10**
*The Living Legend of the Royal Canadian Mounted
Police.* 1957.   **Value: $8-$10**

Modern police yearbooks, usually published on
department anniversaries.   **Value: $20-$45**

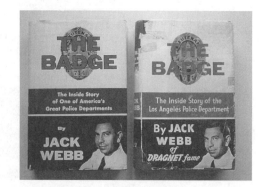

*The Badge-The Inside Story of One of America's Great
Police Departments.* Jack Webb, 1958.
                               Value: $10-$14

*The Badge-The Inside Story of the Los Angeles Police
Department.* Jack Webb, 1959.   **Value: $12-$15**

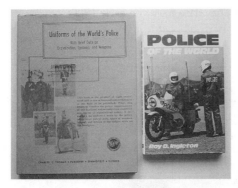

Uniforms of the World's Police. 1968.
Value: $15-$20

Police of the World. 1968.
Value: $15-$18

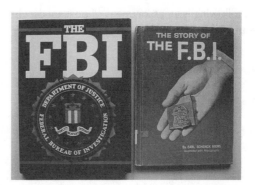

The FBI. 1989.
Value: $15-$18

The Story of the FBI. 1965.
Value: $6-$8

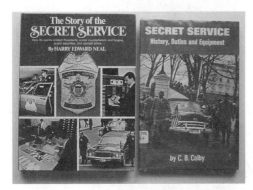

The Story of the Secret Service. 1971.
Value: $12-$14

Secret Service-History, Duties and Equipment. 1966.
Value: $10-$12

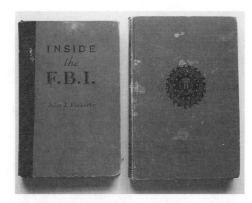

Inside the FBI. 1943. Signed by J. Edgar Hoover
Value: $65-$75

The Story of the FBI. 1954.
Value: $12-$18

The Story of the Secret Service. 1965.
Value: $6-$8

20 Years in the Secret Service-My Life With Five
Presidents. 1973.
Value: $4-$5

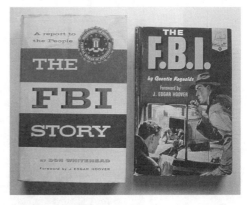

The FBI Story. 1956.
Value: $5-$7

The F.B.I. 1954.
Value: $4-$6

The following is an assortment of post cards with a police motif. They date from the early 1900s.
Value: $.75-$5 ea.

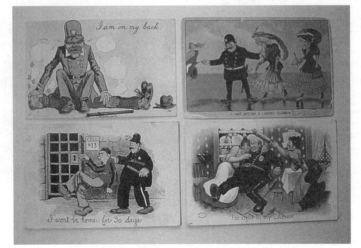

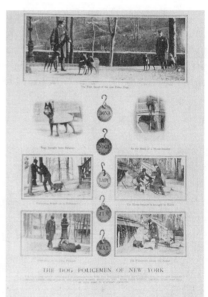

Page from a magazine showing the first police dogs in New York City. The round tags in the center are the original police dog badges which were marked, "Police Department-(dog's name)-New York City."
Value: $12-$18

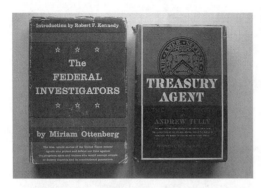

The Federal Investigators. 1962. **Value: $10-$12**

Treasury Agent-The Inside Story. 1958.

Value: $10-$12

FBI Law Enforcement Bulletin (Periodicals) 1939 & 1940. **Value: $12-$15 ea.**

Graduation Program from the FBI National Police Academy-1939. Rare. **Value: $18-$22**

Police agency & association magazines.
Value: $3-$5 ea.

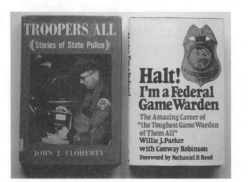

Troopers All-Stories of State Police 1954.
Value: $6-$10

Halt! I'm A Federal Game Warden 1954.
Value: $6-$8

Factory police car brochures. **Value: $8-$20 ea.**

CHAPTER 23

CALL BOXES

The first efficient method of police communications dates back to the nineteenth century when police "call boxes" were used. Chicago was the first city to use the combination telephone/telegraph call box system in 1880. These systems allowed communication, either by signal bell or voice, between the station house and the patrolman on the street. The boxes were located strategically throughout the city so each officer would have one in his beat area. An Indicator Gong, located at the station, would register the number of the call box making the communication which would indicate the location of the officer needing assistance. Although better than no communication at all, there exist many

(Photo courtesy Don Vessey)
Gamewell Police Patrol Box, aluminum alloy with telephone and telegraph sending unit. Late 1920s **Value: $350-$375**

stories of officers having to drag their drunk arrestee several blocks to reach the call box so the wagon could be summoned for transportation of his prisoner.

The call boxes were intended mainly for police use, however, some models had a special "citizen's" key slot. The citizen would retrieve the key from a nearby business to insert into the key slot to report the need for police at that location. The Gamewell Company manufactured fire and police call boxes until the early 1960s and are the type most often encountered by collectors today. Cast iron boxes were made up to 1928, when they were changed to an aluminum alloy construction. The call box is a significant part of police history and a popular collectible.

Gamewell Police Telegraph call box with citizen's key slot. Early 1900s. **Value: $550-$600**

Los Angeles Police call box. 1950s.
Value: $145-$155

Gamewell Police Telegraph call box with wagon call key slot. Circa 1916. **Value: $550-$600**

Gamewell Public Emergency Telephone box. Last style made by Gamewell, 1951 to early 1960s.
Value: $175-$225

Cannon Electric Development Co. Police Signal and Telephone. Made for the City of Los Angeles, circa 1930s. Aluminum alloy.
Value: $375-$395

Gamewell Indicator Gong, circa 1890 -1900 **Value: $4500-$5500**

CHAPTER 24

MISCELLANEOUS

The number of "odds and ends" that can fit into a collection of law enforcement memorabilia is staggering. Virtually any item that depicts insignia, policemen, etc. can be included. These items also serve to set the theme of your display room, which will grab the attention of visitors.

Identification and business cards make interesting collectibles also. Identification cards are most valuable when accompanying an original badge. In days gone by, it was common for police departments to use custom uniform buttons with their department's name on them. Through the years, they gave way to the cheaper 'P', and 'S' marked buttons for uniforms.

Bronze medallion, "CENTENNIAL U.S. SECRET SERVICE 1865-1965" on reverse, "1865-1965 100 U.S. SECRET SERVICE." 2-1/2" wide.
Value: $85-$95

Law enforcement medals and medallions have been made as long as badges, with some examples being quite valuable. Belt buckles of the past are popular and expensive. Hundreds of departments have had custom belt buckles made which some collectors specialize in. These run anywhere from $20 on up, depending on the department and type of metal.

Miniature badges are popular and an affordably priced item. These are usually made in the form of a tie-tac, with a large variety available. Statues of policemen have been produced for many years in many different materials. Bronze statues are at the high-end of the value scale, with toy figures at the lower end.

Police Department City of New York parade belt and buckle. Circa 1900.

Value: $75-$100

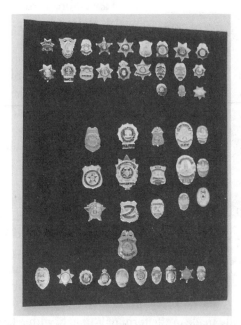

Miniature badges and tie tacs. Miniature badges usually measure 1" to1-3/4" while tie tac badges usually are in the less than 1" size. Virtually all state police and highway patrol badges can be found in miniature size as well as many other city, county and federal pieces. These are very popular and are relatively inexpensive depending on source.

Value: $3-$5

Police uniform buttons. Through the years many departments had custom-made buttons that reflected the department name. Some are still used today but much more common are the generic "P" and "S" buttons, for police, sheriff and security uses. The "P" and "S" buttons have no collector value. Custom buttons.

Value: $2-$3.50 ea.

CHAPTER 25

PERIODICALS AND PHOTOGRAPHS

There are numerous items that serve to set the theme of your display room, which will grab the attention of visitors. Some of the most inexpensive items are magazine covers. *Life, Look, The Saturday Evening Post, The American, Leslie's Weekly, and Collier's* are but a few that have featured law enforcement subjects on their covers. Framed, these make a super display. Good sources for these are flea markets, antique stores, junk shops, which are usually reasonably priced. Obviously, the older they are, the higher the price. Dealers in paper items are a good source also, albeit the most expensive.

Old photographs of officers in uniform are quite popular, most of which are of the "studio card" variety. Buying, selling, and trading of police

Police department group photograph, circa 1930.
Value: $18-$25

vehicle photographs has become very popular in the last decade.

A large variety of books on law enforcement exist also. This area includes old docket/arrest logbooks, old department annual reports, department histories, modern department "annuals," and old training textbooks. Probably all state patrol agencies have done at least one annual/history book. Most major city departments have done likewise. The books usually have nicely embossed covers and high-quality glossy paper like school yearbooks. They show photos of all current personnel and have some historical information as well. These books generally run from $20 to $45. Of a lesser value, but interesting, are old law books.

Magazine covers and advertisements portraying policemen make attractive wall decorations. Values depend on the magazine, it's age and condition.

Value: $12-$22

Policeman cabinet portrait, more valuable when badge is visible.

Value: $12-$14

A ONCE IN A LIFETIME FIND

The great majority of collector's will never find that "once-in-a-lifetime-find." This is a story about one of those rare times that someone actually did, and what they found was a badge belonging to John Behan. For those of you who aren't familiar with that name, here's a little history lesson:

Most Old West history buffs are familiar with the Earp brothers and their famous October 26, 1881, gunfight near the OK Corral in Tombstone, Arizona. In 1881, John Behan was elected the first Cochise County sheriff. Behan was a cohort of the lawbreaking "cowboy" elements in that area. The name "cowboy," at that time, was a derogatory term for rustlers and outlaws. A few such outlaws of the time were Ike and Billy Clanton, Tom McClaury and Billy Claiborne.

During the first Cochise County sheriff's election, Behan convinced Wyatt Earp not to run for the position. Behan, in return, promised to make Wyatt his undersheriff, thereby splitting the lucrative tax moneys they would collect. Wyatt agreed to the arrangement, but after Behan won the election, he named Harry Woods as his undersheriff instead.

Virgil Earp was the city marshal; his brothers, Wyatt and Morgan, along with "Doc" Holiday, served as deputy marshals as needed.

As city marshal, Earp had enacted a new ordinance that outlawed the carrying of firearms in the town limits. The rule stated that when arriving in town, you had to check your guns into the nearest saloon or hotel, etc., before doing anything else.

Behan and the Earps were bitter enemies for many reasons, both political and personal. One example of these problems was Behan's beautiful eighteen year old common law wife who later left him for Wyatt Earp.

The cowboys that Behan assisted, the Clantons and McClaurys, ranched and rustled cattle, with the help of their friends, when they weren't robbing stagecoaches. Tensions grew between the Clantons and the Earps when a secret deal between Wyatt Earp and Ike Clanton (to help Wyatt catch stage robbers) went awry. To cover himself, Ike Clanton started threatening to kill the Earps. After a blow to the head with a gun barrel, Ike was arrested by the Earps for carrying guns in town. Other similar incidents and continued threats led to October 26, 1881, confrontation at the OK Corral.

At approximately 2:30 PM, the three Earps and Wyatt's friend "Doc" Holliday walked toward an empty lot between Fly's Boarding House and the Harwood House, where Ike

187

and Billy Clanton, Frank and Tom McClaury and Billy Claiborne milled around two of their horses.

At least four of the "cowboys" were armed, thus violating the city ordinance. The city marshals were on their way to disarm and arrest them. Sheriff Behan told them that he would go disarm them so there wouldn't be any trouble.

The Earps did not believe Behan and proceeded to the vacant lot anyway. About a half a block from the lot, Sheriff Behan ran up to the Earps and told them not to go down there as he had already disarmed them. The group pushed past Behan and confronted the well-armed cowboys in the vacant lot where the famous gunfight ensued. The end result of the fight was that the Earps killed Billy Clanton and both of the McClaurys. Morgan and Virgil Earp were both wounded, and Doc Holliday received a minor wound to the hip. Now back to the badge…

The following information was provided by Les Bugai, who co-owns the badge with Daniel Geary. The badge is classified a "suspension badge," which means the star is suspended by chains and hangs below the body. The badge is elaborately engraved in Victorian-style, and was probably made by a jeweler from the Tombstone area. It is engraved, "COCHISE CO. SHERIFF" on the face. Behan's name appears in script on the reverse as well as the year, "1881."

Noted author, engraver, and antique arms consultant George Madis has carefully inspected the badge and declares it, "…original and old with no alterations." Master engraver Joseph of Cody, Wyoming, has also examined it and attested that it is handmade and from the time period of the OK Corral shoot-out. Many knowledgeable and reputable collectors have also inspected the badge and overwhelmingly declared it authentic as to age construction, and engraving typical of the late nineteenth century.

In addition, these few ounces of historic silver have been rigorously examined and tested by EMTEC, an engineering consulting lab in Denver, Colorado. Excerpts from their highly-detailed study state, "The badge was examined using the optical microscope at magnifications of up to 140 power. It is our opinion that both the badge and the engravings are characteristic of the late nineteenth century and are deemed authentic."

Using scientific methods and experts in the field are the best way to authenticate a badge.

Beautifully engraved suspension badge that once belonged to Cochise County, Arizona Sheriff, John Behan.

Reverse side showing the name "John Behan" and the year "1881."

COLLECTOR'S RESOURCES

Silver Star Enterprises
Lt. Monty McCord (Ret.), P.O. Box 302, Juniata, NE 68955
Law Enforcement Historian/Author
Buy-Sell-Trade Law Enforcement
    Badges/Patches/Etc.
Law Enforcement Agency badge/patch supplier.

The Last Precinct Police Museum
Sgt. James Post (Ret.), 15677 Highway 62 West,
    Eureka Springs, AR 72632
One of only three privately owned police
    museums in the U.S.
Police Collectibles of all types on display and
    for sale.
Police Car Owners of America world head-
    quarters.

RHS Enterprises
Raymond Sherrard, P.O. Box 5779, Garden
    Grove, CA 92846-0779
Federal Law Enforcement
    Historian/Author/Bookseller
Collect and trade federal insignia; sell insignia
    books on
U.S. Marshals, LAPD, Federal patches, etc.

Firehouse Collectibles
Don Vessey, 4425 Jonquil Ln., Plymouth, MN
    55442
Dealing in Fire & Police Dept. Antiques &
    Collectibles.

In-Pursuit Collectibles
Darryl Lindsay, P.O. Box 412, San Carlos, CA
    94070
Antique police collectibles & patrol car parts.

Les' Antiques & Collectibles
Les Bugai, Jr., P.O. Box 1199
Seguin, TX 78156

BIBLIOGRAPHY

Books

Bondarenko, Mike. *A Collector's Guide to Police Memorabilia*. Police Collectors News, 1996

Brown, Frank and Bruce Davisson. *Worn With Pride*. Brown & Davisson, 1985

Claflin, James V. *Sheriff's Insignia of the United States*. James V. Claflin, 1997

Connors, John J. *Badges of Toledo and Lucas County Ohio*. John Connors, 1973

Cramer, James. *Uniforms of the World's Police*. Charles Thomas Pub., 1968

Gross, T.L. *Manacles of the World*. T. L. Gross, 1997

Ingleton, Roy D. *Police of the World*. Charles Scribner's Sons, 1979

Johnson, David R. *American Law Enforcement: A History*. Forum Press, 1981

Latham, Jr., Frank. *Police Badges Vol. II*. Frank Latham, 1981

McCord, Monty. *A Collectors Guide to USCG Patches*. Monty McCord, 1990

–*Police Cars—A Photographic History*. Krause Publications, 1991

–*Cars of the State Police and Highway Patrol*. Krause Publications, 1994

Nebraska Sheriff's Assoc. *Commemorative History 1894-1994*. Taylor Pub., 1994

Old West Antiques & Collectibles Illustrated Price Guide. Great American Pub., 1979

Prassel, Frank R. *The Western Peace Officer-A Legacy of Law and Order*. University of Oklahoma Press, 1972

Ross, David and Robin May. *The Royal Canadian Mounted Police 1873-1987* Osprey Pub. Ltd. Men-At-Arms Series, 1988

Sherrard, Ray and George Stumpf. *Badges of the United States Marshals*. RHS Ent., 1991

Sherrard, Ray and Keith Bushey, Jacob Bushey. *The Centurions Shield* RHS Ent., 1996

Torres, Donald. *Handbook of Federal Police and Investigative Agencies* Greenwood Press, 1985

Turner, Alfred E. ed. *The Earps Talk* Creative Pub., 1980

Virgines, George E. *Badges of Law and Order*. Cochran Pub., 1987

Police Relics Collector Books, 1982

Articles

Dalrymple, William W. "The Tin Star" *Police Collectors News* (Jan. 1987)

Donoho, Ron. "Legend of the Tin Star" *Police Collectors News* (Oct. 1987)

"Lore of the Tin Star" *Collectors World* (July-Aug. 1970)

Klasey, Darrell. "Monteleone Among First Collectors" *Police Collectors News* (Ap. 1986)

Kogan, Ken. "Signs of the Lawman" *Frontier Times* (Dec.-Jan. 1980)

McCord, Monty. "In the Beginning" *Police Collectors News* (Sept. 1986)

–"Tips for New Collectors" *Police Collectors News* (Mar. 1986)

–"Collecting Military Police Insignia" *Police Collectors News* (Nov.1987)

–"Collecting Reel Cops" *Police Collectors News* (Jan. 1991)

Miles, Joe. "How to Avoid Fake and Repro Badges" *Police Collectors News* (July 1992)

Miller, Burton. "Your Police - Marine MPs" *Guns & Ammo* (Feb. 1974)

Perrin, Tony. "Caveat Emptor - Badge Documentation Tips" *Police Collectors News* (Ap. 1992)

Sherrard, Ray. "Wanted: Police Badges" *Police Product News* (Dec. 1981)

Stephens, Robert W. "Collecting Western Badges" *Relics* (Oct. 1971)

Virgines, George E. "Wild West Badges" *Police Collectors News* (May 1983)

–"Symbols of the Lawman" *Relics* (Aug. 1970)

–"Mark of the Law" *Frontier Times* (Ap.- May 1965)

–"Symbols of the Indian Police" *Real West Yearbook* (Winter 1986)

–"Badges and Badge Toters" *The Westerner* (Issue No. 8)

Young, Alfred J. "Police Memorabilia - The Lure of the Old Time Cops Gear" *The Encyclopedia of Collectibles* Time-Life Books 1979

ABOUT THE AUTHOR

The author began a career in law enforcement in 1974, having served on the Adams and Phelps County Nebraska Sheriff's Departments and retiring with the Hastings Police Department.

When starting out in law enforcement he began a collection of police memorabilia, which consisted mainly of badges. Since 1978, McCord has operated a police insignia business in which he designs and sells badges and patches to many different agencies.

An avid law enforcement historian, McCord published a book in 1982 about the history of the Hastings Police Dept. He has written several articles for *Police Collectors News* on various facets of the hobby. His historical articles have appeared *in The Nebraska Police Officer and The Texas State Peace Officer's Journal.* He continues his collection of police insignia for which he has received "best display" awards at collector's conventions in Missouri, Colorado and Wyoming.

In 1991 his book, *Police Cars—A Photographic History,* was published by Krause Publications. The book was featured in *Autoweek* magazine. In 1993 he graduated from the 174th session of the FBI National Academy in Quantico, Va.

McCord's book, *Cars of the State Police and Highway Patrol,* was published by Krause Publications in 1994. In 1997, he appeared on television in, "The Police Car", which was part two of a three part program produced by A & E's History Channel called, "Wheels of Survival."

He is a member of the Western Outlaw-Lawman History Assoc., the Wyoming State Historical Society, the Nebraska State Historical Society, the Adams County Historical Society, the Single Action Shooting Society, the Police Officer's Association of Nebraska, the FBI National Academy Associates and the Police Car Owners of America.

The author continues his search for law enforcement badges to add to his personal collection.

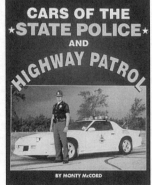
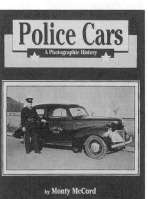

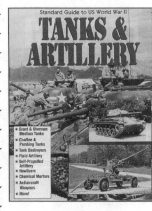